CALL CENTER AGENT MOTIVATION AND COMPENSATION

The Best of
Call Center Management Review

Second Edition

Revised and Updated with New Material!

Brad Cleveland and Susan Hash, Editors

Call Center Press™
A Division of ICMI, Inc.

Published by:
Call Center Press
A Division of ICMI, Inc.
P.O. Box 6177
Annapolis, Maryland 21401 USA

Printed in the United States of America

ISBN 1-932558-02-0

Contents

Foreword

As call centers continue to evolve, so must some of the strategies and tactics managers use to motivate and retain their top agents. That's precisely why we have decided to update our popular book, *Call Center Agent Motivation and Compensation*, with this second edition. In it you will read about some recent trends that impact the way effective managers and supervisors treat their valuable frontline staff, as well as additional information and insights on some more tried-and-true people management practices.

Find out what has worked well in the past, what continues to work and what must change with regard to motivating, compensating and developing call center agents. All of the articles contained in this book were originally published in *Call Center Management Review*, but each features an element of timeliness that makes it as essential to read today as when it first appeared.

We hope you enjoy the book and—more importantly—we hope you're able to incorporate some of the many effective practices into your management approach.

Sincerely,
The ICMI Team

Chapter 1: Motivation

Show us a successful call center that consistently achieves its objectives, and we'll show you a call center that understands—and practices—the key principles of employee motivation. While technology and focused processes play critical roles in customer contact, it's the people behind the machines and work flows that provide the real fuel.

Fancy Titles, More Responsibility Won't Keep Agents

by Fay Wilkinson

Today we have a real opportunity to do things differently. We're used to it; our call centers are breaking new ground every day.

I suspect one of the reasons call center managers consider career paths is to bring legitimacy to our profession. After all, if there's a defined hierarchical structure, then surely we'll be accepted within our organizations? Right? Perhaps.

I suggest we dare to ask: Why do we need traditional career paths? To acknowledge/reward agents for progress? To stop them from leaving? To give them more money/status? To provide variety and prevent boredom? There are other ways to accomplish those objectives. It's time to turn our organizational compass from vertical to horizontal.

What call centers actually need are skilled, energized people who will embrace a variety of new functions with associated skills and knowledge sets. What we want to encourage and value is the development and consistent demonstration of these skills at a superior level. A one-day course does not an expert make. And, yes, as people become more valuable to us we need to pay them accordingly.

So now we're hearing about skill-pathing rather than career-pathing. This fits well with the new generation of "Nexters" coming soon to a call center near you. They are considered to be the most educated generation so far; they are technologically savvy; and their job will be only one factor in their lives, so a fancy title and loads of responsibility may not be high on their priority list.

And no, they won't be staying with you forever no matter what you do. There are some call centers that are being creative, innovative and, frankly, realistic. There simply aren't enough team leader/management jobs for everyone. My hat is off to them. They're on the right track.

Government Call Centers Share Tips for Improving Morale and Motivation

by Leslie Hansen Harps

Improving morale in your call center and providing an environment that meets your agents' needs can pay off in increased employee retention and improved customer satisfaction.

"Truly successful call centers appreciate that call center representatives are the ultimate link to a healthy, productive center," says Terry J. Clements, director of the Social Security Administration's (SSA) Albuquerque Teleservice Center. In the call center, "we have the very strong urge to focus on systems, productivity and management information," he continues. "Yet the real focus should be—and must be—on supporting the people who work with customers in a very stressful environment."

Offering call center employees a competitive benefits and compensation package, while important, simply builds the foundation for happy, satisfied staffers. Other key elements to take into consideration include:

• **Hiring.** All the motivational programs in the world won't help you retain an agent who is poorly suited to work in a call center. Structure your interview process so that it enables you to screen out these candidates. "Using carefully engineered questions that call for specific examples can help you develop insight as to whether or not the candidate has the necessary qualities, such as genuine concern for customers, acting as part of a team, and the ability to learn quickly," Clements says.

The SSA Teleservice Center found that involving management and union reps in the interviewing process "improves the ability to recruit new employees who hold values that are more easily adaptable to the work culture," Clements observes. Some of the things they look for: the ability to handle stress, a sense of humor and flexibility.

It's also a good idea to include in the interviewing process an opportunity for candidates to get a true picture of the environment and what it's really like to work there. This will enable them to make an educated decision about whether or not it's a good match for them.

• **Orientation.** Once you hire an agent, start the relationship off on a positive note with an effective orientation to your organization and to the job. By giving new-hires the information they need to get acclimated, helping them to feel comfortable in the new environment and demonstrating your interest in and appreciation of them, you help to validate their decision to join your organization during the critical first days of the relationship.

"The time to acquaint new employees with the call center's vision, values, mission and culture is immediately," Clements says. He and the call center's assistant manager invest several hours leading an interactive discussion with new-hires on values and expectations of employees, their supervisors and customers. "It helps to get things started on the right foot."

During their new-hire orientation, the New York State (NYS) Department of Tax and Finance, Tax Compliance Division call centers set a positive tone—and demonstrate the call center's importance to the organization. Division Director Joe Gecewicz and other key managers personally welcome the new staff during the orientation and let them know what to expect. So that new tax compliance representatives can be more easily assimilated into the call center, they're hired in small groups of 20.

Another suggestion: Consider assigning mentors or buddies during an employee's first days with your organization to provide guidance and information, and to make your new-hires feel welcome. This can be a motivator for both the experienced agent as well as the new-hire.

• **The work environment.** Also consider the environment in which your agents work, advises John DeFiore. A tax compliance manager with the New York State Department of Tax and Finance, Tax Compliance Division, he oversees two call centers that employ some 300 people. "Problems such as isolation and loneliness, as well as work pace and turnover are common in many centers," he says.

Factors such as these were affecting morale in the NYS call centers, where agents were "bound by a headset, and with minimal opportunity for social interaction." To improve the workplace and enhance morale, the centers took a number of steps, including:

1. Enhancing the work space with new paint and furniture;

2. Combining team meetings when possible to give individual team members an opportunity to meet others within the center; and

3. Actively participating in a very successful department-wide event called TAXPO, an in-house exposition that featured displays from the various units in the department. The event gave call center agents the opportunity to learn about the functions of other units—and vice versa—and helped them to understand where they fit in the overall organization.

• **Training.** Providing continual learning is motivational for teleservice reps and beneficial for the call center. "The better we can create an environment where people are challenged, and provide opportunities where people learn and grow, the more successful we'll be," according to Clements. Both the NYS Tax Compliance call centers and SSA Teleservice Center have dedicated trainers who conduct sessions for experienced call center representatives as well as new-hires.

Recognizing that it can be difficult to fit time for training into a busy call center, the SSA Teleservice Center has established the position of "gatekeeper," an individual who coordinates time for training. "It's not always easy to find the time to train," Clements says, "but you have to develop teleservice reps so that they can grow."

Employees at the teleservice center receive ongoing skills and program training. They also listen to guest speakers or receive training on topics such as celebrating diversity.

• **Career advancement/job enrichment.** As government organizations, the

Chapter 1

NYS Tax Compliance and SSA call centers both have very clear, well-defined career paths. For example, at the SSA Teleservice Center—which has some 600 employees—reps can compete to become a technical assistant, then compete to become a supervisor. In addition to advancing through this career path to management, reps also can compete to move into the center's 50-person claims unit, which gives them broader opportunities for advancement.

In addition, employees at the center can find variety in a number of different ways, Clements points out. "We provide opportunities for teleservice employees to do different kinds of work, such as working in a field office or a contact station where customers are assisted in person rather than by phone." Call center employees are selected to serve on task forces, and to participate in different pilot programs. Reps can also undergo training to become instructors.

- **Rewards and recognition.** The NYS Tax Compliance call centers, like others in the state tax/finance department, are encouraged to recognize the contributions of their peers through Star Awards and Thank-You notes programs. Managers and supervisors can handwrite their commendations using a Star Award, a document about the size of an index card printed with a gold star. The award is given to the individual who performs an extraordinary action, DeFiore explains. Pre-printed Thank-You notes also make it easy for employees to handwrite their thanks to a staff member in any department who has assisted them in some way.

The SSA Teleservice Center has several recognition programs, including a Giraffe Award to recognize individuals who "stick their necks out" to serve a customer. "They can be nominated by peers or their supervisor," Clements explains. Those who receive the award are presented with a small toy giraffe during a special ceremony.

At the Teleservice Center, cash awards can be given to recognize exceptional individual accomplishments. But Clements believes that "providing challenges, a learning environment where the individual feels that he or she has control, and a supporting atmosphere where employees have a sense of involvement, plus friends at work, are much more important than cash rewards."

- **Fun.** The NYS call centers strive to make work fun for their employees. Activities include an Ice Cream Social, as well as contests and special events, such as a Sports Day Dress-Up contest, a Hat Day, Guess the Call Center Stats contest, and Halloween costume and holiday decorating contests. "The contests have proven extremely popular and participation increases with every contest," according to DeFiore. But "while we have made great efforts to make work fun, we have not lost sight of our mission," he says.

Terry Clements agrees. "You can do serious work without taking yourself too seriously." The SSA Teleservice Center has a range of activities that include cookouts, potlucks, functions featuring different types of ethnic foods, Tae Bo classes, even lessons taught by the union president, an experienced folklorico dancer.

- **Management.** Recognizing the significant impact management can have on morale and motivation, managers at the NYS tax compliance call centers agreed to maintain an open-door policy. Managers at one center moved to cubicles placed in the middle of the floor, which improved access and eliminated perceived barriers between managers and the front line.

Managers at the NYS centers also encourage open communication. For example, frontline supervisors solicit ideas from and concerns of their team members during coaching sessions. These are later discussed with managers, with each idea considered and a response given.

Call center staffers can also use suggestion boxes throughout the center. Suggestions are discussed at manager meetings, and a response developed. The suggestions and responses are posted on the organization's Intranet, which was built by frontline staff. The Intranet also contains procedure manuals and resources, plus items of general interest to the call center team.

Managers make a concerted effort to involve staff at all levels, such as when working on the TAXPO, developing the organization's Intranet, or working on procedures. "Managers have empowered our staff to lead in the call center's continuing development," reports John DeFiore. "The staff has responded with many enhancements to the collective work environment." As call center employees' feelings of accomplishment increase, so do the levels of job satisfaction, which leads to increased morale.

Benefits include better attendance and higher occupancy rates. "We're able to handle more calls and provide customer service," DeFiore says. "The many complimentary letters we've received provide the proof that our efforts at improving morale have been worthwhile."

Improving Call Center Performance through People

by Christian M. Ellis and Elizabeth J. Hawk

Call centers drive higher sales and better margins when they are viewed by management as a significant lever of organizational performance.

To gain recognition from upper management, as well as the commitment and loyalty needed from agents, managers have to concentrate on several key areas, such as defining the call center's overall function and mission; developing fair and attainable performance metrics and goals for agents; and developing a compelling employee value proposition.

Define the Role of the Call Center

If you want your call center to be competitive, your agents need to fully understand the mission they're being asked to undertake. For call center leadership, this means clearly stating why their unit exists, what it contributes to the larger business and what appropriate measures will be used to assess its success. In addition, leaders need to develop and communicate a detailed plan for future contribution to the company's overall performance. Without such clarity of vision, the call center cannot hope to successfully compete for the resources and recognition that it will need over time.

Some call centers have been successful in broadening the view of the value they deliver to the larger organization. They can describe their value as: 1) customer relationship management, 2) revenue support, and 3) marketplace sensing to support new product development.

Developing a wider range of success measures allows call centers to reap dual benefits: 1) top management views them as a more critical part of the business, with all the favorable implications for attention and resources; and 2) they are able to motivate their staff with much more engaging missions and goals.

Develop Fair and Attainable Performance Metrics/Goals

A service-oriented center moving beyond the traditional cost-focused "reason for being" will find itself in need of new ways to track performance. In a customer service call center, this might mean moving beyond measures like cost per call, calls handled per hour or average handle time. The productivity focus of these measures is not bad, but it's just not balanced. The drive tends to be viewed as "get 'em off the phone as quickly as possible" and move on to the next call.

SIX TIPS FOR CREATING FINANCIAL REWARDS

There are several rules of thumb in developing financial rewards that drive agent retention and performance:

• Attract necessary talent with a competitive starting rate of pay.

• Provide substantial pay growth opportunity through a skills/ knowledge-based pay progression system.

• Provide flexibility for agents to develop capabilities at their own pace and to focus on areas of expertise that interest them.

• Retain more experienced agents with a competitive living wage.

• Motivate and inspire through focused incentive programs that reward unit/team results.

• Provide significant bonus opportunity for achieving stretch results.

Reps respond well to having the quality (not just quantity) of their work measured. Attention to internal quality measures is one approach, which includes:

• Process compliance checks. Were all of the steps prescribed for the task, in fact, completed?

• Output checks. Did the agent complete the task accurately and was response timely?

Many centers are also adding external quality assessment to their routine measures of performance. This typically involves three steps:

1. Find out what's important to your customers. Is it the speed with which a customer service call is answered? Or do customers care most about getting their problems diagnosed accurately and solved completely? Or is the key whether or not the agent demonstrates empathy and concern for the caller? Note that expectations will vary based on the kind of service being provided to customers, as well as by type of caller.

2. Determine the level of performance customers expect. Is an answer within three rings expected, or is five sufficient? What are the ways an agent can demonstrate the expected level of concern for the customer? Again, these will vary by type of work and by customer type.

3. Find out how agents are currently performing against these standards and how to improve. The call center measures performance, then peels apart its processes and enhances them to meet customer expectations.

Creating a Compelling Employee Value Proposition

Most call center managers would agree that agent satisfaction and retention is directly correlated with customer satisfaction and retention. Yet many frontline employees believe that their company is not doing a good job of meeting their needs.

In a study by Sibson & Co., called *Rewards of Work*, more than 70 percent of frontline workers indicated they were committed to the success of their organization. However, only 51 percent believed their organizations truly cared about their general satisfaction.

Satisfying agents—motivating, supporting and rewarding them in meaningful ways—has become increasingly difficult for several reasons. First, the workforce is becoming more diverse demographically, bringing with it a great diversity of employee needs, values and cultural norms. Second, the workforce is becoming more diverse structurally with full-time, part-time and temporary employees, as well as subcontractors often working side-by-side in one call center. Finally, job opportunities in tight labor markets create a war for talent that makes it easy for agents to "jump ship" for better opportunities.

To improve agent commitment, satisfaction and, ultimately, retention and performance, develop a flexible and differentiating employee value proposition. A comprehensive value proposition clearly spells out the beliefs, policies and practices of the organization in creating a meaningful and inspiring work environment. It also answer the questions "Why do agents want to work in the center?" and "Why should they want to stay?" It involves both financial and nonfinancial rewards (see the Rewards of Work Model illustrated below).

THE REWARDS OF WORK MODEL

People do work for more than just money. The Rewards of Work model shows the five elements of any reward system—two are financial; three are not.

Call centers should address all five elements and find out from their agents what they truly value. Achieving this balanced approach will enable you to differentiate your call center from others, motivate high-performing agents to increase their effectiveness and help to resist the temptation of the (not so green) grass on the other side of the fence.

AFFILIATION
- Organizational reputation
- Company culture
- Work environment
- Corporate citizenship

DIRECT FINANCIAL
- Base salary
- Incentives
- Ownership
- Cash recognition
- Premiums

Rewards
of
Work

WORK CONTENT
- Variety/challenge
- Accountability
- Work schedule
- Meaningfulness
- Performance feedback

INDIRECT FINANCIAL
- Benefits
- Noncash recognition
- Perquisites

CAREER
- Organizational advancement
- Training and development
- Employment security
- Personal growth

Achieving the Right Balance of Rewards

Often, call center pay systems reward people for showing up, staying and working fast, rather than for providing high-quality service and high levels of customer satisfaction.

While there is much talk about variable or incentive pay programs, these approaches will only be successful if other basic rewards are present, including a "living wage"—a paycheck substantial enough to cover the cost of living—and solid healthcare benefits. Keeping close track of wage and compensation trends is critical, especially in low unemployment labor markets where the competition for talent is high.

But a meaningful employee value proposition is about more than just money. It is also about sincerely convincing agents that they belong to a great organization and that their work is truly valued.

This affiliation is easier to sell in some organizations than in others. Some centers may be able to tap into the strong cultural presence of the broader organization. However, others will need to develop employee affiliation within the center itself.

Probably the most compelling approach is to develop a customer-focused culture. Call center agents can more easily get excited about working in an environment that emphasizes customer delight than one focused on maximizing profits for the company. Why? Because they can see the impact on their customers daily but often don't see the bottom-line impact for the company.

Perhaps the most critical step in creating a differentiating and sustaining value proposition is to design work that is meaningful, challenging, has variety and requires teaming or interaction with others.

Improving the work content of jobs is also a great first step in providing a meaningful career element to the value proposition. Studies have shown that agents care about learning new skills, taking on greater responsibilities and strengthening their overall employability.

Perhaps more importantly, they want a reasonably stable environment where they know they will have a job if they perform to expectations. Managers who overlook agent career needs and goals risk high turnover and poor performance.

Bank of America Honors Top Reps at One-of-a-Kind Company Conference

by Greg Levin

In mid-June, Bank of America's (BA) five California call centers lost more than 200 of their best reps for two days. No, their absences weren't caused by a flu that only affects top-performers, but by a unique company conference that honors them.

It's called the "Bankers On Call Conference," which BA developed to recognize agents who provide outstanding customer service and exceed company sales objectives. The conference is held each year at a different hotel in Southern California. During their two days off the phones, the elite agents compete in group games, listen to motivational speeches from senior management, attend an award ceremony honoring the "best of the best," and let loose at an exciting dinner bash. In addition to the agents, at least one manager from each call center attends the annual conference.

While the focus of the conference is on fun, important information is delivered to the agents.

"It's not only a great way to show our top agents how much we appreciate their outstanding performance," explains Diane Pasiuk, conference organizer and manager of BA's Glendale center, "we can deliver messages that are pertinent to their jobs and to their success in the call center. They can then pass this information on to their colleagues when they return to their call centers."

The six California inbound call centers from which attendees are chosen are located in Glendale (which also houses an inbound/outbound sales unit), Orange County, San Bernardino, Pleasant Hill and Fresno. Of the 1,800 agents who work in these centers, 230 were invited to attend this year's festivities, which were held at the Red Lion Hotel in Glendale, Calif., and Paramount Movie Studios in Hollywood. Last year's conference was held at the Hilton Hotel in Burbank and Universal Studios in Universal City.

Selecting Stars, Filling Staffing Gaps

All agent attendees are selected by the managers at their respective centers. Managers determine who the top-performers are based on monitoring results, employee evaluations and general observations of the agents at work. "We look for real service leaders—the agents who go beyond the norm," says Pasiuk. "We consider customer service first, then sales." She adds that top-sellers who don't meet the general service criteria will not be selected to go to the conference.

BA does not have "set-in-stone" criteria or sales numbers that agents must meet to receive a conference invitation. "We trust that managers know who the 'stars' are just from observing them every day," says Pasiuk. "We leave the selection process up to each call center. We don't want to reduce the selection process to, 'You had to have a score of X to qualify.'"

Despite the relatively informal selection criteria, agents seem satisfied with the process. "I have not heard of any complaints about unfair office politics with regard to who gets to go to the conference," says Pasiuk. "It's usually obvious to everybody who deserves an invitation. If we could possibly invite more agents, we would, but we still have a business to run."

And running the call centers without the company's top performers can be a challenge. During BA's first conference two years ago, each call center maintained its normal staffing level by scheduling just enough agents to cover the conference attendees. However, the centers still struggled to maintain their normal service levels. "We had a full schedule, but didn't consider the effect of not having the 'best of our best,'" Pasiuk recalls. "As a result, our handle time went up and we weren't able to take as many calls as usual."

BA solved the problem this year by overstaffing to compensate for the missing top performers. "That worked much better," says Pasiuk.

This Year's Event a Blast for Agents

Those agents selected this year got to travel through time, as the theme of the conference was "Blast to the Future." As the agents piled into the large hotel auditorium for the first conference session, they gazed at a futuristic stage and stars on the walls while listening to Neil Diamond's "We're Headed for the Future" pumping in through speakers.

Don Owen, senior vice president and head of California Statewide Teleservices for BA, kicked off the conference with a talk and a slide show on where BA's call centers have been, how far they've come and where they are headed. While the emphasis was on how the call center technology has evolved and improved, Owen ended his presentation with the importance of customer service and of building rapport with each customer.

The next speaker, Robert Menicucci—executive vice president and region manager for BA—continued the customer service message. Menicucci, who manages many of BA's retail branches, talked about the similarities involved in handling a customer in person at a branch and over the phone at a call center. He reminded the agents that it's important for the company to work together to provide unparalleled customer service regardless of the channel customers choose.

Following a picnic lunch outside the hotel, the agents were split into three groups that rotated through three breakout sessions. Two of the sessions covered BA products and tested agents' knowledge using game show themes. "One of the sessions had a Family Feud theme and the other had a Jeopardy theme," says Pasiuk. "These were rousing, very loud and energetic product knowledge sessions! Agents were leaping around and yelling, bells were ringing. They had a blast and learned while they played." Winners received prizes, including shirts and other giveaways, as well as money.

The third breakout session focused on service and included scripted role-plays of common customer situations. To add a little competition into the mix, agents in each group were divided into teams, with managers rating their performance. Agents were rated on their ability to recognize and take advantage of upselling and cross-selling opportunities, as well as their ability to build rapport with customers. "This session, while not as wild and upbeat as the others, was probably the most important of the three [breakout sessions]," says Pasiuk.

After the three agent groups completed all three breakout sessions, they reunited in a general session. The speaker was Barbara Desoer, group executive vice president for BA's California retail banking division. "Barbara is the most senior person in our California retail structure," Pasiuk points out. "Like the previous speakers at the conference, she talked about the importance of exceeding customer expectations and building relationships with customers. The message was similar to Don and Robert's, but came from a much more senior level. This showed agents that our entire organization is serious about a strong focus on customer service."

Desoer's presentation was followed by a "Q&A" session. Pasiuk admits that she and the other managers had "planted" some questions with agents to ensure that the session didn't bomb, but the managers later found that they had underestimated the agents' curiosity. "The group had so many of their own questions! They didn't need any of ours," Pasiuk says.

Space Suits and Poodle Skirts

In addition to speeches and games, some of the call center managers acted in little stage skits throughout the afternoon to reinforce the importance of customer service. For example, one skit that took place on two stages compared BA's call center past to its future. On one stage, a manager portrayed a character named "Pokey from the Past." "Pokey fumbled around trying to locate a branch, doing all kinds of silly things," explains Pasiuk. "He searched a blown-up map of the world with a magnifying glass in an attempt to find the branch, and interacted very comically with the customer on the phone." The skit then switched over to the second stage, which featured an agent wearing a spacesuit working at a "Jetson-like" workstation. This agent used "Branch Locator" technology to smoothly handle the caller's request. "There were all sorts of funny exaggerations of how advanced our service will be in the future," says Pasiuk. "For example, the technology the agent used not only told him where the branch was, it provided local traffic information so the agent could tell the caller the quickest way to get there."

At the evening event—a dinner/dance party at Paramount Movie Studios—

spacesuits were traded in for leather jackets and poodle skirts. While the overall conference theme was "Blast to the Future," the party theme was "Blast to the Past." "We made it clear to all the agents that the event was going to be strictly social and fun, no business," says Pasiuk. The managers held true to their promise. The '50s theme party included a bubble-gum blowing contest, a hula-hoop contest and a Jitterbug dance contest. Pasiuk was impressed with agents' costumes. "Pretty darn close to 100 percent of the agents got into the '50s spirit," she says.

Honoring the Best of the Best

The next morning, agents traveled back to the present for the final hours of the conference, featuring an agent award ceremony that honored the stars among the stars. Three agents from each of BA's six California call centers (18 agents in total) received recognition for "exceptional performance" during the prior year. Among these winners was an agent who consistently achieves the highest monitoring scores, receives numerous customer comments and helps agents who struggle with service issues. The top salesperson in the state was also among the honored agents. All winners were called up to the stage individually, with their names appearing on a big screen in the front of the auditorium while the song "Best of the Best" filled the room. These agents were each given a clock with a marble base on which their names were engraved.

Don Owen closed the year's conference by reminding agents how important it was for them to take their enthusiasm and knowledge back to the call center. "He told them that we needed them to be ambassadors back at their respective call centers," says Pasiuk.

The agents have done just that. "They [the agents who didn't attend the conference] were very curious about all that happened at the conference when I returned," says Cynthia Salazar, a customer service rep at BA's Glendale call center who attended the Bankers On Call event. "I was able to share what knowledge I brought back."

To enhance the information that attendees passed on to their fellow agents back at their centers, BA videotaped the entire conference for all to see. Pasiuk and other managers edited the video to include the highlights—the key messages presented as well as some of the more humorous and entertaining parts. Team leaders will soon be showing the recently completed video to agents during team meetings and discussing the information covered at the conference. "We put a lot of effort—and money—into the conference, so we want to make sure that it benefits as many employees as possible," Pasiuk explains. "Enabling the agents [who weren't selected] to see what happened increases the value of the conference and motivates agents to work harder so that they have a chance to be invited the following year."

Agents Wowed by Royal Treatment

Pasiuk realizes that she is lucky to work for a company with the funds and call center commitment required to put on such an elaborate conference for agents each year. The agents feel even luckier.

"They are absolutely 'wowed' to be invited to a nice hotel for an overnight event, to be treated royally with great food and entertainment and to get a chance to interact with senior management," says Pasiuk. "They see how much we appreciate the great work they do for us."

Agent Salazar was so impressed she's determined to attend next year's conference. "It was spectacular, she says. "The content was outstanding and I was extremely honored to be able to attend. I am going to do all I can to be invited next year."

Dealing with the "Free-Agent" Mindset: Rethink Recruiting and Rewards

by Susan Hash

The Generation X mindset became a strong force in the workplace in the early 1990s, challenging corporate cultures and rejecting the traditional button-down management policies and procedures.

Just when companies were learning how to adjust to their Generation X workforce (now 24 to 39 years of age), along comes the next wave of call center agents—Generation Y.

Generation Y includes 68 million Americans born between 1977 and 1994 (workers 16 to 24 years of age), 40 million of whom are already in the workforce.

"All of those disconcerting attitudes and behaviors that Corporate America had to learn to work with Generation X have been challenged. It's created even more of a necessary mind-meld for managers to work with the emerging generation," says Eric Chester, author of *And You Thought Generation X Was Tough*, and founder of Generation Why. Chester coined the phrase "Generation Why" to better describe this generation, which "is typified by youth who continually question the standards and expectations imposed by society," (i.e., "why does it matter?" and "why should I care?").

Like the preceding generation, Generation Y is changing the way business has to function and operate, says Chester.

Generation Y can be described as "similar to Generation X—only on fast forward," says Bruce Tulgan, author of *Managing Generation Y* and founder of Rainmaker Thinking Inc., a research firm focused on the working lives of Americans born after 1963. "They're the self-esteem generation. Their independence isn't fierce, it's casual. They know they'll have to take care of themselves and they're not worried at all."

The Staffing Crisis Is Not Going to End

While the Generation Y workforce will surely impact businesses in upcoming years, Tulgan points out that some 20 million older Gen Xers are now managers. "They're already doing things differently," he says.

He adds that the key changes in business were brought about by business leaders and management experts who began to change the employer-employee relationship more than a decade ago through reengineering, downsizing and restructuring. "It's not just young workers who know they have to fend for themselves in this environment. Employers no longer offer job security, so employees of all ages are starting to think like free agents." The free-agent mindset is possibly the biggest challenge that employers have ever had to deal with, Tulgan says.

UNDERSTANDING THE GENERATIONAL PERSPECTIVES

	Baby Boomers 1946-1960	Generation X 1961-1976	Generation Why 1977-1994
The Future	"Is ours!"	"Sucks!"	"Ain't gonna happen.
Wealth	"I'll earn it."	"I don't want it."	"Gimme, or I'll take it."
Employment	"Lucky to find."	"Only if I have to."	"Jobs are a dime a dozen."
Loyalty	"To the end!"	"For a while."	"Until a better offer."
Instruction	"Tell me WHAT to do."	"Show me HOW to do it."	"WHY do I need to know!"
Communication	Via parent's phone	Via personal phone	Pager/cell phone/ email
Change	Dislike	Accept	Demand
Technology	Ignorant	Comfortable	Masters of
Video Game	Pong	PacMan	Mortal Kombat

Source: Eric Chester, Generation Why, Web site: www.generationwhy.com

"That means managing people is going to be much harder than it's ever been. You won't be able to retain people; we're going to have a staffing crisis on our hands forever. Instead, you need to change the way you do business," he says.

Bill Peters, VP of reservations for Outrigger Hotels in Denver, agrees. "There's really no commitment [among younger staff] to the business for the long term," he says. However, he attributes part of that to the job market. "When the economy is down, people tend to spend more time trying to achieve more in their current positions instead of just jumping ship with the first confrontation or poor performance review."

Rethinking Recruiting Strategies

Recruiting is the key process call center managers should consider revamping right away. "In the workplace of the future, you're not looking for people to join the family or climb the ladder," says Tulgan. "Rather, you need people who bring specific skills to the table, who are able to get up to speed quickly and who can begin making valuable contributions right away."

Outrigger Hotels is changing its recruiting process to focus on agents who fit a particular profile—specifically, candidates attending local technical or travel schools, or those interested in getting into the hospitality industry. "We focus on those people trying to get their degrees—sending the message that this would be a great job for them for a year or so," says Sandy Schuster, Outrigger's director of human resources.

"It's not fair to say this would be a great career for you," adds Peters. "But if we can identify that profile during or prior to the interview process, we have a better chance of retaining that employee for at least a year." The call center's goal is to retain 65 to 70 percent of its agents for a year.

Reaching the Right Candidates

Because of the tight labor market, many call centers are so desperate to hire agents that the main selection criterion appears to be whether or not they have a pulse, says Tulgan. Besides changing the recruiting focus to a more short-term

ADDITIONAL RESOURCES

Articles and information on the Gen X and Y workforce are available online:

- Find out more about Generation "Why" at www.generationwhy.com.

- Read about the "free agent" mindset at www.rainmakerthinking.com.

outlook, "the goal of developing a compelling recruiting message and running an effective campaign is to attract an applicant pool that's large enough to allow you to be selective," he says.

At FurstPerson, a call center outsourcing firm in Chicago, recruiting has become a sales and marketing strategy, says Vice President Michelle Cline.

"We've had to take a hard look at the marketing tactics we use to go after candidates in the younger age groups. It has forced us to reallocate some of our resources away from traditional recruiting mechanisms to investing in more Internet and grassroots type of recruiting."

FurstPerson's agent recruiting campaign targets places that Gen Xers and Yers frequent, such as coffee houses, movie theaters and outdoor activities like beach volleyball.

"It does take a little more effort to shake out the right candidates," says Outrigger's Schuster. Her company has expanded its recruiting sources from just using newspaper ads to including radio advertising, job fairs, local community colleges and Internet ads.

An effective recruiting campaign must be both aggressive and year-round, adds Tulgan. "That means all company materials, even sales materials should be developed with your recruiting goals in mind." He offers the following four basic elements and suggestions for developing an effective campaign:

- **Unpaid media (news or quasi-news coverage).** Develop concrete news stories or events to pitch to editors and reporters by building a list of all the potential angles and events that are newsworthy about your recruiting program. Don't dismiss unconventional tactics such as letters to the editor and calls to phone-in talk shows.

BUILD A FLUID TALENT POOL TO LEVERAGE STAFFING ROI

The demand for talent will continue to outpace the supply for the foreseeable future, says Bruce Tulgan. And "there's no doubt that most employers are experiencing the staffing crisis most acutely with their youngest workers."

To combat high turnover, Tulgan suggests call center managers work on developing a "fluid talent pool."

"When agents leave, don't let them leave altogether. Put them in your reserve army," he says. "Offer them the chance to continue adding value on a part-time basis, as flex-timers, telecommuters, periodic temps or consultants. Let them leave and come back in three months, six months or a year." Keep a list of names and phone numbers of high-performing agents. When you have a staffing gap, call your former employees and ask if they would like to come in and work—full time or on a temporary basis.

Then, welcome them back with open arms. "After all," he says. "You've already invested in recruiting and training them, why not leverage your investment?"

- **Paid media (advertising).** The key to an effective ad in any media is being disciplined about sticking to the message. Don't just consider print ads. Write a script for a 60-second radio spot, buy a 30-second spot on cable television or place your ad online at a job posting Web site.

- **Direct contact (mail, telephone, fax, email).** Identify and secure available databases with accurate contact information. Decide which means of direct contact will be most effective for reaching those people.

- **Events (sponsored by you or someone else).** When planning events, keep in mind: 1) What can you do to make the event special to your target market, and 2) What is the potential news/publicity tie-in?

Immediate Gratification Is Key

When it comes to compensation, both Generations X and Y expect to be paid what they think they're worth. The main difference between the younger generations and their Baby Boomer predecessors is the period or intervals at which incentives or rewards are expected.

"These groups don't tolerate annual bonuses or reviews," says FurstPerson's Cline. "They want instant gratification from a financial standpoint, as well as with feedback on performance."

Cline says that bonuses at her company have dropped from yearly to quarterly or even monthly. In addition to monetary compensation, Gen X and Y agents value frequent pay-outs on motivational programs, such as monthly, weekly or even daily.

A roundtable discussion of Outrigger Hotel's agents revealed that, while they like having incentives to shoot for, they prefer those that have monetary value, says Assistant Director of Operations Eric Boyd. "We've offered movie tickets, gift certificates of varying amounts, plus drawings for trips."

What Works Besides Money?

While incentives are great, it takes more than that to motivate the younger workforce, says Chester.

"This is a generation who wants to have contact with a superior to let them know, on an ongoing basis, what they're doing is good."

Also, he says, given the choice between money and flexibility, they would take the freedom—wider parameters, more responsibility, less structure.

Surveys by Rainmaker Thinking found the six top choices of non-monetary rewards among 20-somethings to be:

1. Control over their work schedules.
2. Training opportunities.
3. Exposure to decision makers.
4. Credit for projects.
5. Increased responsibility.
6. Opportunities for creative expression.

"In a call center environment, where it's hard to give agents control over their own schedules, the style of the manager also makes a huge difference," says Tulgan. "Managers need to be right in there, rolling up their sleeves and engaging people."

That's true, says Schuster. Younger agents "are looking more at their managers, making sure they walk the talk—in other words, don't ask me to do something you wouldn't do."

And Bill Peters suggests managers readily accept the questioning they're likely to get from their staff. "There's a lot of thought that goes into that questioning," he says. "It used to be that agents were accountable to their managers. But in today's business environment, managers have to be accountable to their staff."

Chapter 1

Principles of Effective Motivation (Part 1)
by Brad Cleveland

There are countless books, articles and seminars on the subject of motivation. It is among the most popular topics on the professional speaking circuit. Thousands of successful leaders—across dozens of centuries and from virtually every known civilization—have recorded their theories on motivation. And yet some of the most common questions we receive from call center managers include: How can we keep our people motivated; and what are others doing to motivate their employees?

I initially hesitated to write this series. There obviously has been plenty already written and said about the subject. I certainly don't propose to have all the answers. Also—I say this in all sincerity—by looking at the names, titles and companies in our database, we have reason to believe that *CCMReview* subscribers are among the best and brightest leaders in the industry. You haven't built the types of organizations you are part of without being clued in to principles of leadership and motivation.

But the reality remains—motivation is a topic that continues to resonate with call center managers. Can we ever know enough about this topic? And given the ever-changing economy and sense of uncertainty so many employees feel, it is as important as ever.

Consequently, we are enthused about running this series. This first installment summarizes key interrelated principles that drive motivation. I believe in these principles. I have seen them at work in many diverse environments. They are dependable. And they are timeless. They include:

- **Who you are is more important than the techniques you use.** Many programs in management training offer techniques for motivating people—e.g., provide positive reinforcement, celebrate success, create a "fun" environment, etc. There's nothing wrong with using techniques unless they become manipulative—for instance, used solely for the purpose of getting something from someone else. But in a leadership position, who you are as a person matters much more than the techniques you use. Thomas Jefferson once said, "In matters of principle, stand like a rock; in matters of taste, swim with the tide." The reality is, we trust and perform for leaders who are predictable on matters of principle and who make their positions known. Convictions, sense of fairness, consistency of behavior and stated values, belief in the capabilities of people—these things have much more impact than any motivational approach could.

• **People respond to a clear, compelling vision.** A prerequisite to creating a motivating environment is to address the whys and whats—why does the group, team, call center and organization exist? What is it trying to achieve? What's in it for customers? What's in it for employees? Quite a few people have been through the process of creating "vision statements" that, for one reason or another, have had little impact. Nonetheless, a clear focus that is championed by the leader is key to pulling people in, aligning objectives and motivating action.

• **For better or worse, culture is always at work.** Culture—the inveterate principles or values of the organization—guides behavior and can either support and further, or hamper, a motivating environment. Peter Drucker, a noted authority on corporate management and professor at Claremont Graduate School, once said, "So much of what we call management consists of making it difficult for people to work." Creating a motivating environment is often more a matter of what you eliminate than what you put in place—for example, looking for ways to scrap unnecessary hierarchies, cumbersome bureaucracies and "stupid rules" can create a culture that supports and rewards action.

• **Effective communication is essential to trust—and to motivation.** Communication creates meaning and direction for people. Organizations depend on what Warren Bennis, author and professor of Business Administration at the University of Southern California, calls "shared meanings and interpretations of reality," which facilitate coordinated action. When good communication is lacking, the symptoms are predictable: conflicting objectives, unclear values, misunderstandings, lack of coordination, confusion, low morale and people doing the bare minimum required. Effective leaders are predisposed to keeping their people in the know. They actively share both good news... and bad.

- **Fear inhibits action and hampers motivation.** Creating a high-performance culture in which effective communication thrives means driving out fear. This was a theme that renowned management consultant W. Edward Deming spoke of passionately, especially in his later years, and is the subject of one of his famous "14 Points." However, sometimes fear goes unrecognized by managers. For example, agents who are manipulating their statistics and "cheating the system," essentially, may be more afraid of reporting accurate statistics than of "fudging the numbers." That is a symptom of what Deming would have called fear. Of course, there are those things that we should be fearful of, such as the consequences of being dishonest or grossly irresponsible. But it's the wrong kind of fear—such as the fear of taking reasonable risks or the fear of constructive dissent—that we must work to eliminate.

- **Listening encourages buy-in and support.** There is a common myth that great leaders create compelling visions from gifted perspectives or inner creativity that others don't possess. But those who have studied leadership point out that, in fact, the visions of some of history's greatest leaders often came from others. Further, when people have a stake in an idea, they tend to work much harder to bring about its success. Being a superb listener—in big and small ways—pays.

- **People tend to live up to expectations.** It has been proven time and again that people tend to live up to the expectations others have of them. Expect the best and you'll likely get the best. Expect disappointing performance and that's what will likely happen. Think of the people who have had the most positive influence on your life and, chances are, they expected a lot. Those coaches or teachers who believed in us typically weren't ones who were the easiest on us. And they often weren't the kind to win popularity contests. But they believed in us—and we reached a little deeper to live up to those expectations.

- **Sincere recognition goes a long way.** In a study by Dr. Gerald H. Graham of Wichita State University, participants said that the most powerful motivator was personalized, instant recognition from their managers. In other words, being recognized for a job well done. (Other top motivators in the study included managers writing personal notes, organizations using performance as basis for promotion and managers publicly recognizing employees.)

- **Most people have yet-to-be discovered talents.** Writer and editor Elbert Hubbard once said, "There is something that is much more scarce, something far finer, something rarer than ability. It is the ability to recognize ability." This represents a huge opportunity for organizations and for individuals. After all, call centers require more diverse skills than perhaps any other part of the organization. Customer behavior, information systems technologies, queuing theory, forecasting, statistics, human resources management, training, written and verbal communication skills, reporting, real-time management and strategy are all an inherent part of the environment. That call centers lose capable people to environments that are allegedly more interesting is quite an irony. Developing attractive career and skill paths remains a vast frontier of opportunity for many call centers.

- **Conflict will happen; how it is channeled and addressed makes the difference.** In any organization, conflict is inevitable. People need to feel free to express themselves, to vent, to "air things out." Teaching basic conflict management principles can go a long way toward keeping things on track and building a motivating environment.

- **Accurate resource planning is essential.** What does accurate resource planning have to do with motivation? In call centers—a lot! While everyone in the organization may be genuinely "busy," those of us in the call center can't come in early to get a head start on the day's work—nor stay late to handle calls that stacked up in the afternoon. We've got to be there when the work arrives. If we're not, bad things happen: queues build, callers get unhappy, occupancy goes through the roof. It's stressful and, if chronic, it zaps motivation and encourages people to reconsider what they are doing for a living.

- **Actions speak louder than words.** There are countless organizations that post their values, but then encourage an entirely different set of behaviors by their policies and actions. For example, building customer relationships may be the stated objective, but lack of staffing resources or standards that stress volume-oriented production may represent perceived—or very real—conflict in the messages being sent. When it comes to influence, actions always win out over words.

Motivation Principles Are Unchanging

Like leadership itself, effective motivation cannot be bought or mandated. It defies a specific recipe for those who want to create it, and attempts to formulize it often backfire. But the principles behind motivation are reliable, necessary and unchanging.

Principles of Effective Motivation (Part 2)

by Brad Cleveland

While effective motivation defies a specific recipe for those who want to create it, there are dependable, interrelated principles that significantly impact motivation:

- Who you are is more important than the techniques you use
- People respond to a clear, compelling vision
- For better or worse, culture is always at work
- Effective communication is essential to trust—and to motivation
- Fear inhibits action and hampers motivation
- Listening encourages buy-in and support
- People tend to live up to expectations
- Sincere recognition goes a long way
- Most people have yet-to-be-discovered talents
- Conflict will happen; how it is channeled and addressed makes the difference
- Accurate resource planning is essential
- Actions speak louder than words

These principles were summarized in Part 1 of this series. They are universal in application. They are timeless. They are at work in every call center—indeed, in every organization of any type. They must be understood and practiced by anyone in a position of supporting, enabling and leading other individuals (i.e., directors, managers, supervisors, team leaders).

However, the real challenge is in application. In this article, we'll examine five common challenges/scenarios at the organizational level. In Part 3, the final installment in this series, we'll look at scenarios that occur at the individual level.

1. Motivation Begins Outside the Call Center

Our seminars and consulting projects give us the chance to look inside call centers of all types and sizes. Cultures vary widely. Leadership styles run the gamut. And the backgrounds and personalities of individuals working in call centers are wonderfully diverse. Assuming the basics are in place—e.g., a clear mission and direction, reasonable pay and career opportunities, leadership that brings out the best in people—the single most important factor to overall motivation is the call center's value contribution and how that contribution is perceived throughout the rest of the organization.

People are perceptive. When the call center is viewed simply as the department that handles problems, inquiries, or sales—or, especially, when it is seen as a "cost center"—there is an insidious, low-level drain on morale that will defy all other attempts to improve motivation. In other words, the greatest impact call center leadership can have on motivation is often by doing the things that heighten the call center's standing with people throughout the rest of the organization. This goes to the heart of vision, culture and communication. When others see the call center's strategic contribution for what it is, then call center employees will know that what they do really makes a difference. And that will make all the difference in their level of motivation.

2. Even the 'Small Things' Can Undermine Trust

Another major factor in overall motivation is the level of honesty, consistency and trust inherent in the organization. If you're thinking, "Yes of course that's true... but it's certainly not a problem here," don't be so sure.

The vast majority of call center managers I've worked with have unquestionable integrity as individuals, and would be deeply troubled by the notion that anything less than honest was happening in their centers. And yet, seemingly incidental decisions and policies can undermine an environment that is otherwise trustworthy and dependable.

For example, there are plenty of ways agents can "trick the system" to make reports come out in their favor. And they often learn from the best—many managers are producing executive level reports that interpret call center results in such a way as to put the call center in better light than one might find by investigating the details. I know, because I've often been on the other side of the fence, tasked with interpreting these reports to uncover underlying problems and improvement opportunities.

There's rarely an outright intent at either level to "cook the books." But it's important for leaders to be aware of gray areas and minimize the chance that interpretations will vary. Otherwise, a lot of second-guessing will undermine collective confidence—and motivation.

3. Fundamental Question: Is There a Future Here?

ICMI's *Agent Staffing & Retention Study Final Report* noted a host of reasons for agent turnover. The top four included better opportunities outside the organization, compensation issues, better opportunities inside the organization and lack of career opportunities—all of which underscore the importance of developing legitimate career and skill paths.

There are two basic approaches to employee advancement: career paths and skill paths—either can significantly and positively impact motivation. A typical career path model requires the development of job families, which are comprised of a number of jobs arranged in a hierarchy by grade, pay and responsibility (e.g., agent, team leader, supervisor, manager, senior manager, director). Because the historical corporate-ladder approach to staff development can be limited for call centers (due to the finite amount of supervisory and management positions available), a more effective approach may be the skill-path model. Skill paths focus on an individual's acquisition of skill sets. Every call center—even small environments with seemingly limited career path opportunities—can build attractive development and advancement opportunities for employees.

And pay? Many managers are quick to point out that pay is just one factor in motivation, and often not the most important one. But there's a point at which this argument gets carried too far. Pay matters. It does impact motivation and it must be in balance with prevailing opportunities for the skills and knowledge your center requires.

It's quite simple. Advancement opportunities foster motivation. Dead-end jobs erode motivation.

4. Conflicting Objectives are Counterproductive

While few call centers have performance objectives that are diametrically opposed, many do have expectations and standards that are at least partially in conflict, either with each other or with call center realities. For example, the nature of the calls, the processes you have in place, tools available, the skills and knowledge of your agents and other variables determine how long calls should be. If qualitative measurements are refined enough to ensure agents are spending the appropriate amount of time handling calls, then average handling time standards are potentially counterproductive.

Similarly, many of the variables that impact contacts handled per agent are outside of the agent's control (e.g., call arrival rate, call types, callers' knowledge, callers' communication abilities, forecast accuracy and scheduling, coworkers' adherence to schedule). Counting contacts handled per agent as a measure of productivity can also be counterproductive... and demoralizing. Abandonment rate, occupancy and various work-mode quotas are also problematic.

But the other side of this coin is a different world: Objectives that are understood, consistent, fair and that further the creation of strategic value are powerful motivators. Objectives and standards vary widely from one call center to the next. This area represents a significant, ongoing opportunity to further vision, build a supportive culture and establish compelling expectations.

5. Workload Planning is a Significant Motivation Factor

Call center staff can't come in early to get a head start on the day's work, nor stay late to handle calls that stacked up in the afternoon. We've got to be there when the work arrives. We exist in a queuing environment, and being even slightly understaffed during some intervals of the day creates low service levels, high agent occupancy (the percent of time agents are handling vs. waiting for calls), and long queues for customers (see box on facing page).

Understanding and managing the precarious balance between staffing resources and workload is especially important to motivation. The single greatest contribution that some organizations can make toward improving motivation and morale is to improve resource planning and do a better job of matching staff with workload. For example, many tech support reps love working with customers and helping them solve problems. But both become infinitely more difficult when dealing with customers who are frustrated by a long wait to get through. "Those are the days when I can literally feel the tension in my back and shoulders," one person told me. Such workforce management imbalances motivate agents to find work that preserves their well-being, as well as their backs and shoulders.

There's No Single Solution

I'm often asked for best practices when it comes to "motivating employees." The reality is that motivation is largely the result of a systemic, interrelated system of causes that spans everything from resource planning, to objectives, to career opportunities and recognition. There is obviously a lot more to it than pizza feeds or charismatic leaders with a knack at firing up the troops.

SAMPLE BASE STAFF CALCULATIONS

Talk Time: 240 sec; After Call Work: 30 sec; Calls: 150 1/2 hr.

Agents	SL % in 15 sec.	ASA (in sec.)	Agent Occupancy	Avg. Calls Per Agent
23	14%	476	98%	6.5
24	38%	121	94%	6.3
25	56%	55	90%	6.0
26	69%	29	87%	5.8
27	79%	16	83%	5.6
28	86%	10	80%	5.4
29	91%	6	78%	5.2
30	94%	3	75%	5.0
31	96%	2	73%	4.8
32	98%	1	70%	4.7
33	99%	1	68%	4.5

Source: ICMI Inc. Calculations based on Erlang C for one half-hour

Principles of Effective Motivation (Part 3)

by Brad Cleveland

The subject of motivation represents an interesting paradox. On one hand, it is a topic that has been addressed by thousands of successful leaders across centuries. The principles of effective motivation—create a clear vision, establish effective communication, believe in the capabilities of people, lead by example and others—are simple and universal in application. And yet, motivation remains a hot topic among leaders of all types. It seems we can never quite know enough about it, especially in times of change and uncertainty.

Part 1 of this series identified universal principles of motivation, which must be understood and practiced by anyone in a position of supporting, enabling and leading other individuals (e.g., directors, managers, supervisors, team leaders). In Part 2, we looked at common challenges/scenarios at the organizational level. In this final installment, we'll focus on issues that impact the individual.

15 Fundamental Needs

While I am convinced that effective motivation defies specific recipes or formulas, there are definable prerequisites to motivation at the individual level. As individuals, we must:

- Know that our contributions matter—that we make a difference
- Believe in the value of the organization's mission
- Trust the integrity, intentions and competence of those in leadership positions
- Feel equipped and ready to do the work to which we are assigned
- Get constructive feedback on how we are doing
- Believe that our skills, abilities and interests are reasonably well-matched with the job
- Have enough variety in our jobs to keep things interesting
- Know the rules and expectations
- Have clear and accessible channels of communication with executive management

- Believe that we are compensated fairly for our contributions
- Have a reasonable fit (balance) between our work life and personal life
- Work in an environment that is safe and comfortable
- Enjoy a reasonable degree of autonomy in our work
- Have challenging yet attainable standards of performance
- Get the chance to demonstrate and apply our creative abilities

From the leader's perspective, understanding these 15 needs is essential to creating an environment in which motivation flourishes. Together, they should serve as a backdrop to decisions related to employee involvement, performance standards, individual development and other initiatives within the call center.

Employee Involvement

Without exception, call centers that produce the most strategic value for their organizations have a well-defined mission and involve employees in key operational activities that support it. A major precept of the modern quality movement is that those closest to the work know and understand it best. Agents are in an ideal position to help define what constitutes a quality contact, and how processes, training and systems can be improved. Agent involvement also promotes ownership and empowerment, key components of quality improvement and job satisfaction.

Involvement at all levels encourages innovation. As the story goes, James Watt started the industrial revolution by observing the power of steam escaping from a teakettle. This principle still holds true: The most astounding innovations often come from fresh observation of mundane activities right under our nose. I know of an insurance company that redesigned its screen layout based on the ideas of a new agent; the improvements, which no one else had previously thought of, boosted productivity throughout the center.

There are few things as motivating for individuals as seeing their ideas make a positive difference in an organization. Opening channels of communications, encouraging input and following up with communication on those ideas that do or do not get implemented (and why) contributes to a motivating, innovative and rewarding culture.

Performance Objectives

The way in which performance standards are established and enforced has a big impact on motivation—or the lack thereof. For example, using average performance or relative rankings as benchmarks is a potential mine field. It's easy to forget a mathematical principle—about half of any group will perform above average and half below—regardless of the actual proficiency with which the group as a whole is performing. As those below average improve, the average shifts—relegating much of the group to perpetual below-average status. Not exactly a recipe for peak motivation. The same thing is true for relative rankings—one out of every 10 is in the top ten percent, while one is in the bottom 10 percent, regardless of how the group performs.

You can avoid the potential problems that come from using averages or relative rankings by determining acceptable (minimum) performance standards or establishing a sensible range of performance. Either way, getting past relative comparisons will help to avoid a world of potential trouble.

How objectives are enforced also makes a big difference in morale. For example, adherence to schedule is an important performance measurement. But misapplication of real-time monitoring systems, which can measure adherence to the second, can quickly backfire. Today's environment is characterized by empowered agents and participative management styles; yes, schedule adherence is important, but a top-down approach is usually counterproductive. The best approach generally involves educating individuals and teams on the implications of the call center's time-sensitive environment and providing them with the tools and means to track adherence and coordinate adjustments. In other words, monitoring and "enforcement" are moved to teams and individuals as much as possible.

Raising the Bar

Many managers advocate a process sometimes referred to as "shifting performance curves," which aims to turn average performers into top performers. This approach involves identifying competencies (knowledge, skills, abilities, behaviors) of top performers and moderate performers, assessing the gap, and then establishing training needs, performance expectations and relevant objectives to close the gap. The process is designed to actively raise the bar and encourage better performance.

However, this approach must be pursued in the right context. In any group of people, there will be a distribution of talents and skills. Constantly pushing average performers can disenfranchise those who, for whatever reasons, are in the middle of the pack. Further, an age-old complaint workers have against management is that all they receive for good performance is a new set of performance expectations—"No good deed shall go unpunished," as the old saying goes. It can leave people wondering what the rules and expectations really are.

There's a fine line that divides this negative perspective from the positive energy coming from reaching a new goal that you have a part in setting. Leaders who are cognizant of how raising the bar can backfire, typically make an extra effort to involve employees in setting standards. They discourage relative rankings and individual incentives that can undermine the team, and have a good sense of when to migrate performance standards or expectations to a new level. With a participative approach, individuals and teams often push expectations higher than those that would feasibly be established by a top-down approach.

Individual Development

Grooming promotable agents for analyst, supervisory or management positions while they are still agents brings many benefits to those individuals and to the organization. Their interest in the call center environment often increases. They understand the context of their current positions better. They are less likely to look for jobs elsewhere. They are better equipped to contribute to operational improvements and innovations. They tend to inspire their peers to think like managers (e.g., cause and effect, customer retention, bottom-line impact, etc.)

It takes a reasonably structured plan to effectively develop individuals. The plan may include internal and external seminars, participation in crossfunctional planning activities or involvement in special projects. It takes time, commitment and money to develop individuals. But the returns become clear when their unique (and often untapped) talents and abilities begin to blossom—and their enthusiasm for the opportunities that the call center presents becomes evident.

Applying the Principles

Call centers are made up of myriad personalities, goals, skills, needs, etc.—which is why off-the-shelf motivational prescriptions or formulas often eventually fail. For leaders, the challenge is less a matter of "motivating people" and more one of creating an environment in which the motivation already resident in each person can flourish.

As this series on motivation comes to a close, I'd like to suggest some action items:

• Reread the first two articles in the series. You may want to assemble a small, representative team from various roles in the call center and discuss these issues. Identify the areas that need attention.

• Discuss each of the 15 fundamental needs and the degree to which your environment supports these needs.

• Discuss the call center's current major policies and initiatives (e.g., performance standards, skill or career paths, efforts to encourage involvement and others) within the context of the 15 fundamental needs.

• Identify the potential steps that can address these needs while furthering the mission of the call center. Assess the cost, time and effort associated with the proposed steps and develop a plan.

• Identify two or three low- or no-cost actions you can take immediately to enhance conditions that foster motivation. Put them into practice.

There has never been a time when call centers have faced more change—nor a time when we have as much opportunity to positively impact the lives of our employees, customers and organizations. That reality, in and of itself, is motivating!

Chapter 2: Compensation

For years, companies have been touting their call centers as key drivers of customer loyalty and revenue protection and generation. However, as a general rule, organizations have not put their money where their mission statement is. Agent compensation continues to be a source of debate, one mired in myriad benchmarking findings and discussions about how best to measure agents—and the call center's—actual value.

Call Center Professionals Speak Up for Underpaid Agents

by Greg Levin

Lately, everywhere you look there is a business magazine or report telling how companies consider their call centers to be of vital importance–the key to customer retention, increased profits and market share. Companies are investing more in technology and training, and requiring that agents do more to keep up with increasing customer demands. Gone are the days when companies could get away with filling agent seats with mere warm bodies. Today's agents must be able to handle complex call transactions and customer email as well as Web-based contacts, support high-end customer accounts, and participate in numerous important off-phone projects.

So then why are so many companies paying today's agents yesterday's wages?

"Call center agents aren't paid nearly what they deserve. They have one of the toughest and most important jobs in the company, though make less than employees who have positions that are less stressful and require fewer skills," says a call center manager for a bank in Texas.

She's not the only one who feels this way. We have spoken with several call center managers and consultants who think that companies aren't backing up their claims about the value of the call center with adequate compensation for frontline staff–particularly those in non-sales roles.

Companies Ignore Customer Service Agents' Impact on Revenue

"It often takes an edict of God to get a salary increase for customer service agents in most call centers," says Laura Sikorski, managing partner of Sikorski-Tuerpe & Associates–a call center consulting firm in Centerport, N.Y. "Most companies still feel that the customer service agent position is at the low end of the spectrum, just an entry-level position. They don't realize the impact these agents have on revenue." Sikorski points out that a sales rep may bring in new customers with a sale, but it's the support provided by the customer service agent that so often creates customer loyalty and repeat business. "I'm not saying that sales reps don't deserve the good money that they make, I'm saying that management needs to realize the important role that dedicated customer service agents play, and pay them accordingly," says Sikorski.

Few are as impassioned over inadequate agent compensation as Mary Beth Ingram, president of the call center training consultancy Phone Pro (see her article, "A Candid Conversation on Call Center Compensation," later in this chapter).

"As the role of the call center has evolved, the job classification and resulting pay scale of the frontline staff—the people who we ask to know the most in the call center—has lagged behind," says Ingram. "I believe that wages for call center agents are woefully low and must be re-evaluated."

Ingram alludes to a study conducted by the Society of Consumer Affairs Professionals in Business (SOCAP) in 1997 to support her claims that customer service agents deserve better compensation. According to the executive summary of SOCAP's *Consumer Loyalty Study*, call centers "not only excel in delivering service quality, but are significantly affecting the consumer's future buying patterns." (Ingram explains that consumer affairs call centers are typical of many customer service centers—they handle mostly compliment, complaint and inquiry calls from existing or prospective customers.) Specifically, the study revealed that the typical consumer affairs agent contributed an average of $1,359,745 per year of what SOCAP refers to as "lifetime consumer loyalty dollars." The value of a typical phone call from a customer to a consumer affairs call center was found to be $95.

Ingram points out that many consumer affairs calls are about small-end products like toothpaste, food items, etc., and that, therefore, $95 is probably a low figure for call centers that support higher-end goods and services (computers, banks, etc). Even still, she gladly uses the figure uncovered by the SOCAP study in her calculations.

"Say your typical agent handles 50 calls a day—a conservative number," says

Ingram. "That agent handles $4,750 ($95 x 50) a day for the company. In a week, the agent handles $23,750. In a year, $1,235,000! And we all know that it's not uncommon for agents in many call centers to handle 100 calls a day or more. The point is that the amount of loyalty dollars to which frontline staff contribute is astounding, but these figures are overlooked by most senior managers."

Given these numbers, how much should a qualified customer service agent be paid? Ingram's response: a wage/salary more comparable to that of sales staff. To get a rough idea of what this might be, she suggests taking the $1,235,000 figure previously mentioned to determine how much of that a typical outside sales rep would be paid. Average commission for sales reps is about 5 percent, meaning that they would receive $61,750 a year. "Even if we give experienced customer service agents only 3 percent commission," Ingram explains, "they would still be making more than $37,000 a year. That's a darn sight better than the $17,000 to $20,000 that most are making now."

Like Sikorski, Ingram isn't trying to reduce sales reps' salaries. "I don't have a problem with sales staff making a lot of money—they work hard to earn it. But let's pay the customer service folks—the people who are in the position to ensure years of repeat business—what they are truly worth, too."

Poor Payment = High Turnover

The most damaging effect of inadequate agent compensation is the high employee turnover so many call centers experience. While many managers acknowledge that low pay isn't the only cause of attrition, they claim it is the reason most commonly cited by agents leaving the center. At many call centers, agents even make lateral moves to what managers say are less-challenging though higher-paying jobs in other departments within the company.

"During exit interviews, agents often tell us, 'Hey, I'm taking a promotion for an easier job in the company,'" says the Texas bank center manager cited previously. While frustrated by the attrition, she says she can't blame the employees. "Why should an agent want to work his or her heart out in the call center for $8 or $9 an hour if he or she can work in a department that is less stressful, provides similar opportunities for advancement and pays $11 an hour?'"

Basing agent pay on what benchmarking results and salary guides suggest is not a solution to the problem of poor agent compensation, she adds. If the majority of companies don't pay agents what they are worth, why mimic them?

"I've been to several meetings with managers of other bank call centers where we discuss numerous issues—particularly compensation—for benchmarking purposes," she says. "But the problem is that none of our companies are paying agents what they deserve. I've told colleagues at these meetings, 'Unless some of us get agent pay up, we're all going to be stuck in this benchmarking loop and continue to underpay agents, which will cause high turnover to continue.'"

In addition to causing existing agents to flee, the mediocre pay at many call centers makes it difficult to attract qualified applicants to replace them, leading to poor service and even more turnover. The resulting high cost of training and retraining agents should alone be enough to compel senior management to increase frontline wages, says the bank manager, but management just writes high turnover off as a necessary cost of having a call center.

What is most frustrating to her is that management doesn't understand how essential agents are to the overall financial success of the organization. Regardless of whether or not they are involved in selling, agents at the bank have their fingers on the pulse of much of the company's revenue every day, says the manager, and their compensation should reflect that.

"Agents have a crucial, valuable job. They need to know a tremendous amount of information and are responsible for providing excellent service to retain highly valuable credit card accounts. But without offering decent pay, it's hard to find and/or hold on to the kind of people who can do those things well."

Rather than just complain about the compensation/turnover problems at her call center, the manager is currently reviewing them with senior management at the bank. "We are raising awareness about the value of agents and the cost of turnover, which will hopefully lead to positive change."

Agents Still Viewed as "Operators" at Financial Service Call Centers, Says Manager

Andrew Pohlmann, call center manager for Old Kent Financial Corp. in Grand Rapids, Mich., agrees that customer service agents' crucial role in customer and profit retention is underplayed, and says they are underpaid as a result. "Most financial services call centers originated from backroom operational areas," he says. "It's difficult for management to take the leap and say that customer service agents are no longer operations workers, they are customer contact workers who are in the trenches and are as important to revenue as the frontline sales reps. Instead, customer service agents are still viewed as 'operators' and paid accordingly."

Convincing senior management to increase customer service agents' pay is a challenge because management wants to see clear-cut data on revenue generated by those agents, says Pohlmann. While information like that revealed by SOCAP's Consumer Loyalty Study can help in this regard, tying customer service agent performance directly to revenue retention/gains for senior management to see is difficult. But that doesn't mean that call center managers should throw in the towel.

"You need to do everything you can to impress upon senior management that customer service agents are valuable assets, not liabilities," says Pohlmann. "It isn't easy, but you need to try to break it down to dollars and cents and say, 'This is how much we pay agents now; this is how many transactions they conduct; this is what a typical customer relationship is worth, and this is what it costs to retain that relationship.'" Presenting that type of data can help you convince management to "do the right thing" and increase salaries, he says.

While it may be easier to link revenue gains to sales agent performance than to customer service agent performance, that doesn't necessarily mean that call center sales agents are paid what they deserve either, says Pohlmann. "Our sales agent compensation is pretty good, but I think they should get paid more considering the revenue they generate." He points out that sales agents in the call center are paid roughly the same as sales people in the bank branches, despite

Chapter 2

55

the fact that end-of-the-year reports show that call center sales agents generate three to four times more revenue than those in the branches.

Not an Enticing Career Move

Bank call center managers aren't the only managers frustrated by unfair agent compensation. For example, a group of seven managers/supervisors at a recent small group forum were asked, "If you were an agent, would you want to work in your call center?" Five said "no." When asked why, the primary reason given was "inadequate compensation for the work done."

Paying agents what they are worth would not only attract qualified agents to the center and retain them longer, it would encourage those with a passion for the work to make a true career out of being an agent, says one manager of a telecommunications call center.

"Not everybody wants to become a manager or executive at the company. There are many employees who would love to make being a customer service agent a career if they could make a decent living doing so. So why not make that an option and pay 'stars' a premium? Just think of the power of the call center's front line if among it were agents who loved what they do and were truly dedicated to providing the best possible service they can. But the way they are paid now, they can't look at it as a career, just as a job."

Pizza Parties Don't Pay the Piper

As important as it is to fight for fair agent compensation, consultant Sikorski warns that pay alone doesn't ensure service quality, high employee morale and low turnover.

"You still need to use creative rewards and recognition, and involve agents in interesting projects to avoid burnout," she says. "Agents need some fun injected into their often-repetitive jobs and want to know that their input is valued by the company."

But Sikorski is quick to point out that such motivational tactics often aren't enough to keep agents striving to dazzle customers. Good financial compensation needs to be worked into the mix. "You can have as many pizza parties as you want," she says, "but after awhile agents are going to want to see their performance reflected in their paychecks."

Getting senior management to change its tune on agent compensation won't happen overnight. Call center professionals must continue to demonstrate the influence their frontline staff has on customer loyalty and revenue generation/retention. The answer to "what should we pay our agents?" should not be determined by merely looking outside at what other companies are doing; the focus should be internal, based on what your agents are worth to your company.

Chapter 2

Agent Compensation: Motivating Staff without Burying Budgets

by Dan Coen

Unlike professional athletes, even superstar call center agents are unlikely to go on strike if given the option. However, the needs that drive pro athletes are not any different than the needs that motivate agents to perform at their very best. Agents recognize the same basic tenet of compensation as athletes: Money drives performance, and performance is expected to drive money. Agents expect to receive quality compensation for quality work. While they don't expect to be paid like star baseball players, they do expect to be rewarded fairly and consistently based on fair market value.

Designing a compensation plan for call center agents can be tricky. Pay is the most critical element because it drives stability and performance. Yet pay is not the only component of a successful compensation plan for agents. Incentives and time-off often play a part in compensation plans that succeed long term. Team vs. individual bonuses and base salary vs. commission should be explored, too. Agents claim that without such elements, management doesn't make compensation exciting, and thus fails to turn it into a source of motivation.

The Principles of Agent Compensation

In my experience, I have found that there are seven principles that should be considered when implementing an effective agent compensation plan:

1. The compensation plan must be centered upon a company's ability to pay. Every company is different when assigning a certain percentage of pay to its agents. An independent customer service call center may not provide the same type of compensation agreement that a Fortune 500 firm will. Management must be cognizant of how much money and investment the company can make in the call center.

2. The compensation plan must be centered upon demand. Developing a compensation plan in the heart of a large city is quite different from coordinating a plan for a small-town call center. Many part-time agents located in small college towns are typically available only seven months out of a year, with little competition for their services. They receive an hourly wage and incentives if applicable. Full-time employees in major cities are available 12 months a year, but competition from other employers is steep. They usually receive a package that includes base salary and incentives based on company performance, if applicable. If management in a small town changes their compensation plan based on each season, they may risk alienating part-time agents who wish to work all 12 months. Similarly, continuous compensation adjustments in a major city may cause retention to suffer.

3. The compensation plan must be centered upon job requirements. While the basic concept of an agent position is the same, the job duties are always different. This means that management cannot mimic other compensation plans because each company has different objectives. A compensation plan must be centered on the objectives of each particular job. Issues to consider include, "What skills does an agent use on a daily basis?" "How does this role differ from other roles in the organization? "What type of candidates are we looking to attract?"

4. The bond between management and agent must be based on trust. The more confusion about pay, the weaker the bond. Agents feel entitled to show a lack of commitment if management flip-flops on compensation issues. They feel a loss of confidence in their superiors, all of which leads to higher turnover. If the objective of management when designing a call center compensation plan is to discourage turnover and enhance the relationship between agent and manager, the plan must be developed correctly the first time, and implemented with a long-term approach in mind.

5. A compensation agreement must be based on appropriate performance objectives. Managers may pay their agents based primarily on one or two objectives, only to learn that other objectives are more critical to the call center's success. If an established agreement leaves open any doubt about measurements or objectives, the compensation plan will falter. For example, a sales-oriented call center should compensate agents more for sales production than for overall agent availability.

6. Pay agents based on what you want them to make, regardless of industry averages. Managers may base their formulas on published compensation tables in trade magazines and newsletters. This is a mistake. If an agent accepts a position at $7.50 per hour and a monthly team bonus, then the agent assumes this is how compensation for that job works. Just because a compensation table portrays paying a part-time, inbound agent X amount per hour doesn't mean your agents may not accept something less—or demand more. I encourage management to create their standards for a position. The needs of one company may not work for another.

7. Don't be afraid to play with BIG NUMBERS or create unique standards. This opens the door to creative compensation. For example, suppose 100 full-time agents in your call center earn $9 per hour. What if you paid them $8 per hour? What if you took the savings ($800 per day, $4,000 per week, $16,000 every month) and applied it to measurements that could reward every agent with far more then their basic $9 each hour? To illustrate, suppose the most important objective in your call center is available time. At the moment, 30 percent of your agents have available time of between 75 percent to 100 percent. Budget the $16,000 you saved for 50 percent of agents to meet the goal of available time between 75 percent to 100 percent. If 50 percent of agents meet their goal next month, they each get a $320 bonus, which is $160 more than they would have received if they had their basic compensation plan of $9 per hour. If only 40 percent of agents meet the goal, then there is even more money to go around ($400 per agent), or more money to spend next month. Management now has created a compensation plan that rewards call center agents for doing what they are required to do anyhow. This plan excites agents to meet objectives that must be met. Agents feel motivated when presented the opportunity to strive for something unique.

Chapter 2

Agent Input Is Essential

Merely following these seven principles is not enough; you must find out what agents want to secure a comprehensive compensation plan. Conduct focus groups with agents to get their input. The alternative to not asking for agent feedback is to develop a plan that falls short of doing what you need it to do.

Develop a survey that asks agents various questions on compensation. Keep in mind that questions like: "Would you like a higher base salary?" won't tell you anything.

Instead, try questions like:

- "Would you take a smaller base salary to possibly earn more compensation in bonuses, commissions and incentives?"
- "Is it important to you that management provides consistent prizes, awards and incentives to complement a compensation plan?"
- "Would team bonuses and bonuses in addition to your salary based upon measured goals motivate you less than a simple compensation plan that relies on individual performance?"

Creative Compensation: A Delicate Balance

Call center managers face several obstacles when designing an effective compensation plan. They must ensure that agents are compensated fairly for their work without exceeding budgets. They must also ensure that agents feel continually motivated to perform at a high level.

Too many managers stay within safe confines when developing compensation plans. While this may ensure fairness, it often limits opportunity and excitement. However, some managers become so involved with creativity and opportunity that they fail to develop a plan that produces measurable results. By developing a well-founded and inspiring compensation agreement that serves specific objectives, agents become a partner in ensuring success for your company.

A Candid Conversation
on Call Center Compensation

Mary Beth Ingram is president and founder of Phone Pro, an Indianapolis-based call center consulting firm that specializes in providing soft skills training for frontline staff. As a speaker, she is a perennial favorite at call center conferences.

Question: Whom do we ask to know the most, but often pay the least in the call center?

Answer: The frontline staff.

What you are about to read is a personal perspective on phone rep compensation. It is based on 12 years of observations in more than 100 call centers spanning a wide variety of industries and applications. It is my own view. Some will agree with it. Others will take issue with it.

Compensation is a touchy, sensitive issue. There are wonderful exceptions to cite where compensation is commensurate with the requirements and talents of the staff. For example, my hat goes off to the consumer affairs profession that, in my opinion, leads the way in fair compensation for call center professionals. But even this accolade is not 100-percent true for all consumer affairs applications.

As a trainer and consultant, I have had the privilege of working in small to gargantuan call centers—small, as in fewer than 10 reps; gargantuan, as in 1,400 reps. The industries vary from a scientific research help desk to a moving company dispatching center; from healthcare and insurance customer service to consumer debt collections; from order entry for footwear, to computer technology hotlines; from utility companies to car companies; from consumer affairs for beverages to consumer affairs for household cleaning products. The calls range from the simple to the complex; from less than a minute in talk time to 20 minutes in problem-solving time. The callers are from the broadest spectrum you can imagine, with questions and concerns that run the gamut of trivial to criti-

Chapter 2

cal. This is the broad base from which come my observations on rep compensation.

Rep Pay Scale Lagging Behind in Evolving Industry

When you look at the evolution of the call center, you see tremendous and positive change. The roots of the call center go back to the "plain vanilla customer service department" of the 1960s and 1970s. This was first and foremost a support function. Its primary mission was administrative tasks with a secondary mission to answer the phone. Customer service representative, secretary, file clerk and order entry clerk were the titles you found there. Contact between the customer and the company was mostly through the outside salesperson, and the consumer was not yet much of a player.

The power of the consumer developed in the '70s, built steam in the '80s and exploded into a force to be reckoned with in the '90s. As this has occurred, the plain vanilla customer service department has given way to the call center. Now there is often a call center for consumer affairs and one for customer service; one for new accounts and one for collections; one for the help desk and one for dispatch. Call loads continue to grow. Technology advances. The primary mission of a call center is to answer the phone to serve the customer or consumer, and the secondary mission is to do administrative tasks (now mostly PC-driven). That's a complete flip from where the industry began.

The call center has become the pulse of the organization, the corporate service center, the nerve center, the one-stop shop dream! How envious sales, marketing, communications, public relations and other departments have become of its resources, talents and access to the buyer. Many call centers are profit centers and are adding revenue to the corporate balance sheet.

But as the role of the call center has grown and evolved, the job classification and resulting pay scale of the staff has lagged behind.

I'm Willing to Be the Renegade!

I believe that, in most organizations, wages for call center reps are woefully low and need to be reevaluated. This includes taking a look at incentive programs, which are sometimes used not to enhance and increase someone's earnings (although that's how the program is sold), but to keep wages artificially depressed through a set of questionable, usually subjective, standards.

Think about what call center reps can do. In most centers, they are skilled at operating multiple computer programs, many of them custom applications. Reps are able to read and assimilate instantaneous packets of data from the computer about buying history, demographics, account numbers, history of past conversations, alerts for credit problems—all while conversing coherently on the phone.

Reps take in a constant stream of information from reader boards on current ACD stats, not to mention messages flashed about the special of the day, reminders to cross-sell and upsell, items in back-order status, items overstocked that need to be moved at discount. Reps interact with a wide spectrum of callers from either the consumer or the customer side of the business. They possess an excellent working knowledge of company products or services. They maintain a firm grasp of company knowledge as it applies to procedures and policies. They know the organization well enough to gather appropriate resources for the customer and to serve as their advocates. Many are proficient in current promotional activity, support outside sales representatives, and even manage entire territories in some instances. They interact with marketing, credit and shipping, and are active participants in call center project teams, all the while completing the administrative and followup work necessary to satisfy the consumer or customer and the boss! Outside salespeople often are not as well-versed and resource-ready as the average call center rep.

The list of rep "duties" may be less or it may be more in your call center. Now look at your requirements for a position in your center. Have they stayed the same or are they getting tougher? The days of "must like to talk on the phone" as a job requirement have often given way to "must have a college degree."

The Paradox of Incentives

What about incentive programs? When tied to sales productivity, incentives can be great, and success is easy to track. When the measure is more illusive, incentives can be demoralizing. I witnessed a rep get "scored" low because the coach determined the rep did not offer enough options in the call. Never mind that the rep sold the caller the product quickly and effectively with the first option presented. That coach's determination cost that rep $1 per hour for a 40-hour week on an hourly wage of $6.50. Scoring is always objective in the real world: baseball, hockey, golf, bridge tournaments. Isn't scoring low in a subjective environment really "opinioning" low? Anyone who is serious about coaching and interested in the personal development of his or her staff knows intimately how fine the line is.

What about incentives for stats (e.g., goals for number of calls taken, talk time, after-call work, availability)? At a glance, these incentives seem logical. What if you get the luck of the draw and the ACD decides to send you all the problem-resolution calls and your neighbor gets simple orders or inquiries? What if you are asked to participate in a meeting or must troubleshoot a situation for a customer with the marketing department? What happens when the balance of quality and quantity is affected by the drive for 50 cents more per hour on your paycheck? And if management makes allowances for all the special circumstances, who gets the tedious job of tracking it all when they could be supporting the frontline staff or talking with escalated callers?

Outsourcing Creating "Third World Wage" Strata?

Early on I stated that the consumer affairs industry is often the exception in this area. It has led in the compensation game with higher earnings and salaried positions. But outsourcing is changing the landscape for consumer affairs as well as for other call center applications.

Far too many frontline staff at outsourcing companies are paid in the $6 per hour range. A conversation I had not too long ago with someone working at an outsourcing company revealed he had just secured his position at $7 per hour, which was 50 cents higher than the outsourcing firm he had worked for across town. He had a college degree, was married with one child and held another job to make a living. His call center job required him to be proficient in computer technology and Internet software.

And yet, outsourcing is not a "cheap alternative." That's not why a company chooses to go outside. The decision is more complex, more strategic and, in fact, a major expense item. My fear is that the frontline job in outsourcing is creating a sort of "third world wage" strata.

Check Should Reflect Respect

Well, what's the bottom line? I simply desire to see the call center profession garner more respect, not just in verbal and written appreciation of what the call center means to the company, but in the paychecks of the folks who make it happen, who are asked to be the first voice and image, who are required to be trained and knowledgeable, who encounter the best and the worst of humanity on a daily basis, who are probably in the call center because their desire to serve is their strongest trait. Perhaps for one day, just one day, all call center frontline staff should stay at home. Count the lost revenue from sales and the cost of lost good will. Then get the executives down to the call center to answer the phones, and we may just find the budget for wages and salaries increased to reflect the talent and skill required for the job.

Chapter 2

Agent Compensation Strategies Reflect Changing Job Roles

by Susan Hash

As the call center's strategic role within the organization continues to evolve, so, too, has its compensation strategies. Traditional pay models may become obsolete as the labor market rebounds and call centers are, once again, faced with tight competition for skilled agents.

Although a stubbornly soft economy has kept the lid on pay increase budgets for the past few years, employers are attempting to differentiate the pay increases awarded to their top, average and low performers, according to a compensation survey by Mercer Human Resource Consulting. Mercer's survey shows that, across industries, the strongest performers will receive average pay increases of 4.8 percent in 2004, compared to 3.1 percent for average performers and 1 percent for the weakest performers.

"In the current environment, employers need to be concerned about their high-performing employees and those with critical skills," says Steven Gross of Mercer's U.S. compensation consulting practice. "These are the employees they need most to help the organization pull out of a difficult economic period. Unless you reward these employees at a sufficiently higher level, you risk losing them when the economy gets better. If you can't accomplish this through base pay increases, other actions may be needed to retain and motivate these valuable employees, such as incentives and rapid career growth."

Skills Development: An Alternative to Promotion

For call centers, a longtime impediment to agent retention has been the perception that it's a dead-end job. Among call center job seekers, 45 percent feel that there is a below-average number of opportunities for career advancement in the industry, according to a survey conducted by Call Center Careers. In the typical call center, it often comes down to a numbers game. "There are certainly opportunities for career growth for agents within a call center, but from a ratio standpoint (number of agents per supervisor) you're never going to be able to satisfy all of the career-oriented individuals," says Bob Gills, CEO of Call Center Careers.

Because traditional career path opportunities are limited in many call centers, some companies are adopting an approach involving skills-based progression and pay. And, in fact, the complexity of the agent's job and variety of skills required makes skills-based development and pay an effective, and successful, strategy.

"Eighty percent of the training and coaching applied in contact centers is product and system navigation training," says Elizabeth Ahearn, president and CEO of The Radclyffe Group, a customer interaction consulting firm based in Whippany, N.J. "Typically, only 10 percent of the training budget is allocated for skills training, yet skills training reduces the stress of the job and keeps people intellectually challenged."

A typical skills-based pay program enables agents to master up to three or four skills per quarter. As they demonstrate proficiency in various skills, they receive small raises over the course of a year as opposed to one low raise at the end of the year that doesn't relate to what they're doing, she says.

Putting Agents in Charge of Their Destiny

About four years ago, ADP's (Automatic Data Processing) Employer Services division, a provider of integrated outsourced payroll and human resources services, adopted a skills-based pay and reward system as part of its transition from a dedicated rep environment to a team-oriented one, says Deb Hughes, vice president of Human Resources, Eastern Division of Major Accounts of Employer Services. The program involves a series of skills training and assessments at three agent levels: Level 1, new-hire; Level 2, nine to 12 months on the job; and Level 3, 12 to 18 months' experience (while these are the typical timeframes to reach proficiency at each level, an individual's movement through the levels can be accelerated, Hughes says).

To advance and earn pay increases, agents must pass a series of evaluations testing their product knowledge, strategic interaction skills (i.e., call strategy) and ability to use the tools available to them (e.g., the call center's client management system). In addition, peer assessments evaluate agents' ability to work together as a team.

"Instead of being on an annual merit increase schedule, agents can earn accelerated increases above what they would traditionally get as a merit increase—and even what they might get from a merit increase and promotion," says Hughes. "It puts agents in control of their own compensation, which was one of the original goals."

And agents appreciate being in control of their own destiny. Since the program's implementation, retention in the call centers has risen to more than 80 percent. In addition to retaining motivated, growth-oriented staff, the program helps those who may not have an affinity for call center work to realize it early. "It's so much easier when people identify that for themselves than when managers have to do it," says Hughes.

Because of its success in the Employer Services call centers, ADP is currently developing similar skills-based compensation programs for its other divisions. "Merit increases, especially in this economy, are not very motivating," Hughes says. "Our agents see the value of going through a program that involves acquiring knowledge to pass various evaluations. Being evaluated also becomes a reward because, if they do well, they feel good about it and they gain recognition among their peers. We really don't have to sell the program; it sells itself."

Sales Incentives Boost Agent Pay and Bottomline

Offering sales incentives is another way call centers are putting agents more in control of their paychecks. Some call centers are finding that converting a service center into a service and sales center is lucrative for both agents and the company.

A service and sales program implemented at Lavalife Inc.'s call center increased the company's annual sales 21 percent, or $15 million. Lavalife is an

Chapter 2

independent provider of technology-based dating services for singles, with its primary call center located in Toronto, Canada, and annual sales of $75 million. Lavalife uses Web-based and IVR technology to enable singles to meet other singles anonymously by recording and exchanging messages or via a live one-on-one connection through the service.

Lavalife's philosophy was customer-oriented, says Nancy Major of Design 7 Consulting, who was given the challenge of turning the 100-seat call center into a sales center within three months. "Customer service was first, with no assertive attempts to close or offer customers the product. The customer calls they were receiving were really gifts—gifts that they were not recognizing. Any time a customer calls you, they're saying "Hey, I am interested in your product or service. Tell me why I should want it.""

A conversion to a service and sales environment requires a fair and rewarding incentive plan that can be measured and monitored, Major says. "It's critical to have the systems in place to track, monitor, measure and report the results at the individual, team and product or service level."

The program Major set up for Lavalife was a simple, entry-level type of system that included fair, attainable stretch objectives. "It has to be a relatively simple program to measure and for the staff to understand and embrace since they're in control of the outcome," she says. The objectives were set on a sliding scale based on agent experience level—newer agents with less experience were given lower sales conversion objectives than those with more tenure and product knowledge.

Of course, transitioning from a service focus to a sales environment is not without obstacles. Over the six-month launch, Lavalife lost two managers and 20 percent of its agents. "Not everyone will embrace a change of direction from service to service and sales," Major says. "Call center staff require a ramp-up period and a lot of coaching through the process—and that should be a key performance indicator for the management team so that it's not taken lightly."

Recognition Is a Valuable Incentive

Recognition plays a hefty role in any compensation program's success. Continual promotion of cross-selling and upselling successes at IBM.com's call centers keeps its service agents motivated to generate sales leads. The organization's 2,000 service agents are trained to recognize certain words or phrases that indicate a customer is interested in a purchase, says Rich Vazzana, IBM.com's vice president of Support and Enablement.

Once identified, opportunities are then warm-transferred to a sales agent who will close the sale. IBM.com's opportunity management system tracks opportunities identified through a six-step sales process to the closed sale. The number of leads produced is one of the key performance indicators considered in service agents' annual performance appraisals and pay increases, along with customer satisfaction, calls handled, call quality and other service metrics.

In addition to annual appraisals, service agents are continually recognized publicly for their contributions to sales. "We hype it up," Vazzana says. "At department meetings, we read customer appreciation letters, announce how many customers were forwarded for opportunities and how many were closed by individual agents, and congratulate them in front of their peers." Besides recognition, agents also receive $25 or $50 awards for outstanding performance in generating sales leads.

IBM.com's service agents, first and foremost, are there to resolve the customer's issue, Vazzana says. However, he adds, "the service agents are ecstatic that they're able to help the sales process through. As long as they feel that the work they're doing in this environment is important to the management team and to customers, they're motivated to keep doing it."

Investing in People Pays Off

For many call centers, bolstering an archaic pay system will require a sea change in senior executives' views of the role agents play in customer loyalty, says The Radclyffe Group's Ahearn. She cites customer lifetime value research conducted by the Center for Client Retention, which found that, over a five-year period, an agent has an impact of $1.3 million on the business.

Within the center, Ahearn adds, managers "need to stop spending their time putting out fires, and start investing in their people from a time and emotional standpoint. Agents are our product, and we need to invest in developing and improving our product."

SERVICE CENTERS LAGGING IN MANAGEMENT INCENTIVES

Agents aren't the only ones being incented to increase sales. A new study by research and consulting firm LIMRA International found an increased focus on sales incentives for contact center managers, as well. But the amount—and, ultimately, the effectiveness—of the incentives varied by type of contact center, says Senior Research Analyst and Project Director Malcolm McCulloch.

The sales incentive for management of sales centers was typically 10 percent or greater of base salary, an improvement over past years where it was generally below 10 percent. "For incentives to work, they should be at least 10 percent of base salary," McCulloch says. "Below that, it really won't influence behavior."

Management sales incentives for service centers fell below the 10 percent mark, which McCulloch attributes to the heritage of the service environment. "The service world comes from a different background and compensation philosophy than sales centers," he points out.

The study tracked management incentives at three levels: 1) Corporate (e.g., profit sharing), 2) call center performance, and 3) individual performance. More than half of sales and service contact centers (55 percent) offered management incentives at the corporate level, based on how the company performed.

At the call center and individual levels, sales centers again outpaced service centers for management incentives. Twenty-seven percent of sales centers offered management incentives based on call center performance, versus 19 percent of service centers. Eighteen percent of sales centers offered incentives based on individual performance, while only 12 percent of service centers did so.

Source: 2003 Compensation Survey for Contact Center Management, *LIMRA International,* *www.contactcenter.limra.com*

Chapter 2

Chapter 3: Incentives

While paying a competitive salary is critical to attracting and retaining the best agents, call centers need to add a diverse range of incentives and rewards—both monetary and non-monetary—to the compensation mix to keep agents intrigued and in place. There is no set formula for what works in regard to agent incentives; it often depends on the specific needs of your individual call center and staff. However, the articles in this chapter describe several common practices and strategies that most centers with successful incentive programs incorporate.

Use Incentive Programs to Link Desired Behaviors with Rewards

by Leslie Hansen Harps

Incentive programs "are intended to link the behavior of individual employees to the types of performance that you need in the organization," observes Gerry Ledford, practice manager of employee performance and rewards for Nextera's Sibson Consulting Group in Los Angeles. Incentive programs in some call centers achieve only lukewarm results or, worse, backfire and reinforce the wrong kind of behavior, while others exceed expectations.

"Incentive programs that are aligned with customer satisfaction, have clearly identified performance standards and are consistent" can work very well in the call center, says Anne Nickerson, principal of Call Center Coach, Ellington, Conn. She cites a successful call center incentive program in a highly complex financial industry in which the goal was to improve the accuracy of information given to customers. When the incentive program was implemented, all the necessary tools were put into place, including clear standards and expectations, a system that provided accurate information, training and "mini-trainings" for the call center agents, and a monitoring and coaching process. Reps who performed well became peer coaches and all coaches were trained and calibrated to ensure consistency in their evaluation.

Unfortunately, many call center incentive programs "tend not to be very well-implemented and often are not very well-designed," Ledford says. Probably the single most common problem of design, he says, is failure to use a broad enough measurement base. "You need a balance of measures to reflect the different kinds of performance you want from people. Otherwise, you'll sub-optimize."

Design an incentive program that rewards productivity only, such as handling more calls in an hour, and your service quality may suffer. But if you incent only quality, Ledford says, "you almost certainly will see productivity decline."

A well-designed, well-implemented incentive program may have as many as

Chapter 3

three to five variables, or even more, he says. Finding the right mix and balance is one of the keys to a successful program.

Broadening Measures

Boston Coach, an executive sedan service, revamped its incentive program to increase the number of measures, reports Nancy Leeser, vice president of international reservations and customer service for the Boston-based company. "When we first introduced the incentive program," she explains, "it was based purely on quality," measuring number of errors per transaction. CSRs who met their goal received an incentive of 5 percent of their salary. The program was deemed to be too subjective, and "we weren't sure we were getting our money's worth," Leeser says.

A supervisor in the call center worked with CSRs to develop a revised incentive program through which reps can earn up to 5 percent of their salary. "It's a multifaceted program," Leeser says. To determine the categories, "we selected the things that were important to us in running the business." Reps earn points in the following categories:

- Individual attendance and punctuality.
- Schedule adherence.
- Number of transactions.
- Level reached in the company's career pathing program (with number of points awarded increasing as the level increases).
- Improvements in number of service failures for the center as a whole.

Depending upon overall point total, a CSR can earn a 100 percent payout, a 50 percent payout—or no payout at all.

"We are getting what we hoped for" from the program, says Leeser. Implemented last year, the program was fine-tuned this year, combining attendance and punctuality into one category and moving to a quality measure that rewards group, rather than individual, performance.

Rewarding with Recognition

In addition to its corporate-wide recognition programs, the service area of Independence Blue Cross (IBC) uses a multifaceted recognition program called "Blue Diamond."

"It's a monthly program that recognizes our service reps," explains Hank Kearney, senior director of member service for the Philadelphia-based company. The program keys in on four areas:

- Attendance and punctuality.
- Accuracy and professionalism, as determined through monitoring (reps must receive a rating of 99.5 percent or more).
- Performing at "expectations-plus" in categories such as staff time, after-call work and follow-up work.
- Going above and beyond the call of duty.

Contributions in the last category are noted by a rep's supervisor, says Roe Tabasco, manager of quality assurance and training for IBC. For example, a rep may have helped to train others within the unit, handled special projects with timeliness and accuracy, worked overtime, received complimentary letters from members, made suggestions for improving work operations or simply may have been an enthusiastic, motivated coworker.

Blue Diamond awards are given out on the last Friday of each month on "Blue Diamond Day." Reps who have earned a Blue Diamond receive a certificate, a blue diamond to put on the certificate and a gift voucher for the company cafeteria. The number of individuals who receive Blue Diamonds varies, with perhaps 10 to 20 of the 225 service reps at the call center recognized each month.

Once a year, a recognition breakfast is held for the top Blue Diamond winners. These employees receive a certificate, an American Express gift certificate and a gold coin (part of the company's corporatewide recognition program).

The program has been in place for more than five years and is very successful, Kearney says, especially with reps who are making the call center their career.

Chapter 3

Balance Service and Productivity

When developing an incentive program, suggests Gerry Ledford, first define what role the call center plays, then identify key measures that support the role. This will enable you to tie rewards for the individual to the type of performance you want from the call center. For example, "if you don't see the call center as a sales channel to reach customers and expand the business, then rewarding cross-selling is a waste of time," he says.

Use a balanced mix of metrics, Ledford advises. For example, a productivity measure, such as number of calls per hour could be balanced with a metric from customer satisfaction surveys or measures of individual quality. It's crucial not to reward productivity at the expense of service quality, or vice versa.

"Productivity is a lot easier to measure than quality," according to Nancy Leeser. "You have to put your money where your mouth is on the quality piece, going out of your way to reward quality." Boston Coach does not include "number of phone calls handled" in its incentive program, she says. "We reward things which lead to that—if you're in your seat adhering to your schedule, you will take more phone calls. But we've never given a target number of calls reps need to take in a day."

Independence Blue Cross intentionally does not include a productivity category in its recognition program. "We want to send the message that we'd rather have it done right the first time, so we do not emphasize the reps having to take a certain number of calls, or having a certain average talk time," says Hank Kearney. "I'd rather have a rep with a higher talk time who delivers quality service—one who's leaving customers 'wowed'—than a rep who moves customers in and out quickly."

A Learning Opportunity

For an incentive program to change behavior, it's important to combine it with coaching—particularly when it comes to service quality, says Anne Nickerson. She describes an ideal incentive program as one that has "clear, consistent rewards tied to improvement in behavior, with opportunities for every-

Chapter 3

one to understand and learn what that behavior is and looks like."

This would include giving call center agents feedback immediately after a call and letting them know what they can do to improve their score, as well as their management of the customer. "Deliver the feedback in a way that's very specific," Nickerson advises. "Give examples, models and approaches that the person can use" to improve his or her performance.

An incentive program combined with coaching will get better results, agrees Gerry Ledford. "People tend to act as if you can announce an incentive plan, turn on the switch and it will work. That's not the case. You have to do all the hard management labor of communicating, training, reinforcing, monitoring and coaching" to get the results you want.

"It's quite possible to get unintended results, to unintentionally reinforce behaviors you don't want," he says, so it's critical to monitor the incentive program to make sure you're getting the results you expected.

What Type of Reward?

"All things being equal, dollars are going to be more effective than praise" as a reward, according to Ledford. "While different things have different reward value for individuals, almost anybody is going to find money motivating." The question is, how much money does it take to drive a change in behavior?

"The available evidence suggests that an incentive becomes powerful when it represents 5 percent to 10 percent of base pay," Ledford says

"Money is one incentive, but there are many more," observes Anne Nickerson. "I also see incentives that are fun, which helps improve morale." At one call center, for example, agents who earned a certain number of points could put leaves on the branch of a tree. Each completed branch was worth so many points, which could be turned in for rewards such as massages, manicures and pedicures, free pizza and certificates at the local mall. Agents loved the program and the prizes.

At a health care and financial services call center, Nickerson says, when agents met and maintained a specified quality goal, managers would make and serve

Chapter 3

breakfast or serve reps an afternoon treat from a fully equipped snack cart. In another call center, an entire team that cleaned up a database earned a trip to Las Vegas by "beating the clock."

Whatever reward you decide to use in your incentive program, remember that "the more often you reward behavior, the more often you'll get it," Ledford says. Monthly or quarterly incentive programs are the most common. If the time horizon is longer than that, the program is less likely to reinforce the behavior you're seeking. So make sure there's lots of communication and publicity to keep interest high.

A DIFFERENT LOOK AT INCENTIVE PROGRAMS

"To me, delivering a certain level of quality and efficiency with productivity is how you keep your job," notes Donna K. Richmond, president of the Richmond Group, a customer service consulting firm located in Wheaton, Ill. "I think that an incentive should be for above and beyond the call of duty."

Richmond has strong feelings about incentive programs in the call center. "The goals have to be a real stretch, but they also have to be reachable." She cites the case of one call center paying a base salary of $20,000, with a potential incentive payout of as much as $10,000. "But the incentive was nearly impossible to get," Richmond says. "Once the agents realized it wasn't do-able, they either quit or stopped trying."

She also suggests that managers examine whether or not they can achieve the results they desire without an incentive program. "Can you get the same or better results by paying people more money, and getting more talented, more experienced people?"

Finally, she advises, don't treat the incentive program in a vacuum. "If you're monitoring people for the program, take advantage of the opportunity to look at the whole picture." Examine the process and root out barriers that may get in the way of agents doing their jobs.

Chapter 3

Are They Worth It?

Incentive programs that are designed and implemented well can pay off handsomely. Gerry Ledford cites a study conducted by the American Compensation Association. The study, which looked at 660-plus incentive plans across a range of industries, identified the net return on payout as 134 percent. "That's for an average payout of three percent," Ledford says. "Typically, the higher potential for gain, the higher the success rate." Companies in the most successful quartile in this study had a whopping net return of 378 percent.

While there have been some whopping failures, on the whole, incentive programs are quite successful, Ledford says. "And they're one of the most successful types of intervention you can come up with."

Chapter 3

Air Canada's Agent-Run Incentive Program Flying High

by Dan Coen

When it comes to staff motivation and incentives, Air Canada's Vancouver reservations center relies on a team of proven experts—its own agents.

"A team of call center agents plans and administers all of our contests and incentives in the call center," says Butch Gregoire, manager of customer service and reservations for the Vancouver center, one of Air Canada's five reservation centers in Canada. "We felt it would bring accountability to the staff and add more fun for the agents if their own peers were involved in the coordination of our motivational efforts. Agents have their finger on the pulse of our center, so they are the natural people to create incentives for everyone."

The agent-run incentive program began in 1996 with six reservation agents comprising the Incentive Committee. Prior to the formation of the committee, morale had been good, but not energized, says Gregoire. Managers and supervisors did their best to foster enthusiasm and spirit, but their other duties hindered their ability to create an incentive-oriented environment. "Agents motivating agents" was a logical step.

Providing Peers with Inspiration and Information

The Incentive Committee's six members are dedicated to developing and promoting contests and prizes for fellow agents in the call center. All incentives are product- and knowledge-driven, helping to educate agents while inspiring them to perform.

"Our biggest challenge as a committee is identifying contests or incentives that meet three goals," explains Vanessa Coad, an agent who has been on the Incentive Committee for two years. "First, any contest must not get in the way of performing our primary job, which is providing service on the telephones. Second, everybody must be given an opportunity to participate in each contest. Third, each contest must teach our agents something new, whether that entails

Chapter 3

sales skills, product information or computer training."

Being a member of the Incentive Committee is a job all its own, says Goad, who originally joined the team to help bring some excitement to what can be a mundane job. Every two weeks the committee meets to discuss future incentives and contests, and to coordinate the rules and promotion of events. They are each assigned duties, ranging from organizing prizes and awards to developing promotional materials and regulations.

To help them plan accurately for their audience of 131 reservation agents, committee members constantly encourage feedback. Questionnaires and surveys are handed out to agents twice a year, and nearly 100 percent are returned and tabulated. Using the feedback of their peers, the committee develops the various contests and incentives.

The committee receives a small amount of money from the company to help fund the various incentives. "We provide them with a limited budget," says Gregoire, "so they need to be creative when choosing prizes if they are to succeed in motivating the other agents. They have done quite well establishing relationships with hotels, restaurants, movie theaters and retail stores around Canada."

A Closer Look at the Committee's Creations

One of the most successful contests the Incentive Committee created was "Victoria Day Escape." The contest, which took place during Victoria Day, the Canadian national holiday that falls on the third Monday in May, featured one very simple objective: book flights to the city of Victoria. To help motivate agents during the contest, the Incentive Committee created posters and fliers promoting the city of Victoria and posted them around the call center.

Each time an agent booked such a flight, his or her name was placed in a draw-box. Entries were unlimited and names were drawn weekly. Winners received various prizes including gift certificates to local restaurants. At the end of the three-week contest, one name was drawn for the grand prize—a two-night stay in one of the finest hotels in Victoria, airfare included.

Another successful contest created by the Incentive Committee was the "Air

Canada/United Airlines Codeshare Challenge." Air Canada has a working agreement with United Airlines to service passengers looking to fly to or from cities/countries not serviced by Air Canada. The Codeshare Challenge contest was intended to enhance Air Canada agents' knowledge about United Airlines. For example, agents took quizzes on United's hubs and destinations. Agents who did well on the quizzes qualified for prizes, such as gift certificates to clothing stores and restaurants.

"This was a big tournament for our department because it lasted for weeks and met our objectives for fun and knowledge," explains Goad. "Agents particularly enjoyed it because plenty of prizes were given away." Agents also competed to generate the most revenue during the Codeshare Challenge. Prizes were awarded for things like most tickets booked for applicable cities and most electronic tickets sold.

Not all contests in the call center run on such a grand scale. For instance, the popular "Tip Box" contest rewards agents who submit the best sales skills or product information tips to help their colleagues. Winners receive gift certificates to movies, restaurants or retail outlets.

Quality and Union Issues Top List of Challenges

While the agent-run incentive program has been a big success at the Vancouver reservations center, there are some challenges. For instance, finding time for meetings can be difficult for Incentive Committee members. Because they work different schedules, the members sometimes find themselves trying to play catch-up in order to put together quality programs. "We have trouble sticking to our meetings every two weeks, so two or three of us often get together on a spur of the moment and begin planning," says Goad.

Another challenge the Incentive Committee faces is effectively working educational aspects into each contest. For example, one contest—"Sing for Your Supper"—features agent groups who sing "Oh Canada" at the front of the call center whenever they meet certain sales objectives. While this contest is fun for agents and adds levity to the daily grind, it isn't as educational as other contests, such as "How Literate Are You?" where agents write a 250-word essay using as many Air Canada terms and as much product information as possible.

Perhaps the biggest challenge Air Canada has had to overcome regarding its agent-run incentive program is the fact that the reservations center is unionized. The union initially had serious concerns about the program. "They didn't see why agents should be congratulated for doing a good job at the expense of other agents when they should all be doing a good job anyhow," Gregoire recalls.

Gregoire and his staff explained to the union that motivation and incentives are critical to call center success, and that putting agents in charge of the program was the optimum way to put together the best programs for all agents. But it wasn't until the union leaders saw the program in action that they gave their support. As Goad explains, "Once the union observed how well our contests and prizes had motivated the other agents, it became a huge supporter of what we do. The union has even talked about featuring our results in an annual newsletter that it produces for its members."

Success May Spread Enterprisewide

Due to the success of the agent-run incentive program at the Vancouver center, Air Canada is considering implementing the program enterprisewide. This would involve forming a national incentive committee of agents responsible for developing contests for all centers. "It's close to a reality," Goad explains, "but the implementation is intricate and will take some time. It's hard enough developing incentives for and motivating 131 reservation agents; on a national scale with more than 1,000 agents it would be even more complex."

Whether or not the program goes national, Gregoire knows that it will continue to help his agents excel and take pride in what they do.

"Many of our 131 agents were caught in the normalcy of the daily call center world before the Incentive Committee was formed," he says. "Now they have new life. It is quite common to hear agents who have been with the company 15 or 20 years say how much fun they are having each time they arrive to work because of the contests, incentives and prizes."

Incentives that Rev Up and Retain Agents

by Leslie Hansen Harps

Good incentive programs benefit both the employee and the organization. They can excite and energize call center agents, and improve morale, quality and performance. And they can help call centers retain their best agents—a crucial benefit in today's tight labor market.

But a poorly designed incentive program can backfire, create disgruntled employees and negatively affect service and quality. Planning and managing an incentive program begins with ensuring that it is aligned with your organization's—and your call center's—culture and mission. This means that, if you are committed to delivering top-notch service, your incentive programs should include a balance of quality and quantity components. Over-emphasizing "the numbers"—i.e., number of calls handled per shift—can cause quality and service to suffer.

It's also important to consider your incentive program through the eyes of the people it is designed to reward: your call center staff. Otherwise you may find that the very activities meant to spark productivity, service and morale may actually hamper them.

And while "soft" rewards like ice cream socials and "thank you" certificates from supervisors are important, they should comprise just one part of an overall reward and recognition program. Agents need to feel valued, and need to feel that their contributions are recognized throughout the organization—by senior management as well as by other departments.

Finally, incentive programs should reinforce and supplement solid compensation and benefits—they cannot be a substitute for them. This article assumes that agents are paid fairly and competitively.

What Do You Want the Program to Push?

Call center incentive programs can be used to:

- Reward performance or effort that has already taken place;

Chapter 3

- Motivate improvement in individual, team or call center performance; and

- Encourage change in agent behavior, such as reducing absenteeism.

Designing an effective call center incentive program begins with identifying precisely what you want your program to accomplish. Do you want to recognize individual accomplishments? Strengthen team spirit? Drive improvements in service levels or quality? Do you want to recognize performance after it occurs (via "spot" awards, for example) or spark improvement in future performance?

Whatever your specific goals and objectives, you need to make some important decisions before designing your incentive program:

1. Rewarding the few or the many. Singling out one or a handful of winners is great for those who win, but it actually can be demoralizing for the majority of agents who don't.

RESPECTING DIFFERENCES

Effective incentive programs take into account generational, cultural and individual differences among employees. What motivates one agent may be a turn-off for another. For example, a study conducted by F-O-R-T-U-N-E Personnel Consultants studied "baby-boomers" (born between 1945-54); "baby-busters" (1955-64) and "Generation Xers" (1965-74). Each group's top reason for staying with a present employer was different:

- Opportunity for career advancement was cited by 51 percent of Generation Xers as a reason to stay (compared to 36 percent of baby-boomers and just 22 percent of baby-busters).

- The work environment was the top reason for staying put for baby-boomers.

- Work/family balance was the No. 1 reason for baby-busters.

Using a mix of rewards can help meet the needs of today's workforce. Training that leads to greater employability may be a great motivator for Generation Xers, while baby-busters might prize time off or rewards that can be used by families as well as individuals.

Source: www.towers.com

Consider balancing individual award programs such as "Agent of the Month" with programs that are designed to reward a larger percentage of the group. Some incentive programs are designed to make everyone a winner whenever someone achieves a certain level of performance or completes certain tasks. An important side benefit of these programs is the sense of community and team spirit that they foster.

2. Individual vs. team. Incentive programs can be used to recognize individual or team achievements, and to spark individual or team performance improvement. There are pros and cons of each approach.

All-team programs in which everyone's contribution is recognized can demotivate high performers who may feel that their individual accomplishments are not appreciated. All-individual programs, on the other hand, can result in excessive competition among agents that can be harmful in a team setting. That's why many incentive programs feature a blend of individual and team rewards.

3. Monetary vs. non-monetary rewards. While cash awards can be popular, evidence is mounting that cash is not always the greatest motivator. One study, conducted by the American Management Association, found that incentives which help employees improve their skills—such as technical and interpersonal skills training—were considered more effective motivators than immediate financial rewards.

According to American Express Incentive Services, "when companies try to motivate employees with an extra paycheck, the award dollars typically go toward the necessities: laundry detergent, diapers, car payments. But non-cash awards—gift certificates, debit card-type awards, travel and merchandise—leave participants with tangible reminders or fond memories of their hard work." The company cites a three-to-one return on investment in non-cash rewards compared to cash rewards.

The best way to find out what will motivate your agents the most is to ask them. This can be done using a survey (which should be anonymous) or via team or staff meetings.

Once you learn what motivates your agents and decide to incorporate non-

Chapter 3

monetary rewards in your incentive program, you can have great fun identifying potential rewards. Examples include:

- Points that can be accumulated to earn merchandise
- Fun contests (such as one modeled after the television show, "Who Wants to Be a Millionaire?" with service- and product-related questions and creative prizes)
- Paid time off
- Tickets to movies, sporting events, concerts or plays
- A day at the spa
- Big-ticket consumer items, such as a television, personal computer or home entertainment center
- An all-expense-paid trip or weekend at a local hotel/resort
- Certificates, trophies, plaques
- Dinner out for two, with baby-sitting services provided as appropriate
- Special meals (such as a lobster dinner) delivered to the agent's home
- Group food functions (such as a barbecue, picnic or pizza parties)
- Celebrations (such as an awards dinner)
- Parties tied to the theme of the incentive program, such as a tailgate party

Because different things motivate different people, effective incentive programs often enable agents to select their rewards from a menu of prizes or feature a combination of cash and non-cash rewards.

Disarm De-motivators

For an incentive program to be fully effective, it's important to identify and minimize/eliminate those things that can potentially de-motivate agents.

De-motivators can range from a bleak working environment to constant time on the phones; from low rates of pay to excessive paperwork; from a slow computer system to lack of respect from senior management or poor response from an interfacing department.

What de-motivates your agents will vary from person to person. But chances are good that there are some overall things that frustrate and de-motivate nearly everyone. One way to identify them is to include a question about de-motivators when soliciting agent feedback for your incentive program. Then do something about it.

12 Steps to Develop an Effective Incentive Program

Regardless of the type of incentive program you decide to implement, follow these 12 steps to make sure that it motivates and energizes agents and gets the results that you seek:

1. **Identify goals and objectives of the incentive program.**

2. **Put together a team that will plan and design the program.**

3. **Develop the planning process and schedule.**

4. **Identify budget for the year.**

5. **Review previous reward and recognition efforts, and research other call centers' experiences.**

6. **Seek employee feedback through team or staff meetings, focus groups and confidential surveys.** Find out what motivates the greatest number of people, and what the de-motivators are.

7. **Design the program so that it meets your goals and objectives.** What will the criteria include? Should it reward individual and/or team performance? Will it be inclusive or selective? How will potential equity and popularity contest issues be addressed? What will be the process for nomination and selection? How will the awards be distributed? Get professional advice on any tax and legal issues.

8. **Test it out to make sure that it will get the results you seek.** Solicit feedback from agents, team leaders and supervisors. View it through the eyes of the employees who will participate in the program.

9. **Revise the program as necessary.**

10. **Develop a communication strategy that covers how you will announce the program, maintain interest, announce the winners, etc.** Put together supporting materials, including answers to frequently asked questions.

11. **Roll out the program.** Watch it carefully. Try to keep interest up through-

Chapter 3

out the program. If participation lags, find out why.

12. **Evaluate results.** Did you get the results you expected? If not, why not? Seek agent feedback: What did they like, what didn't they like? Incorporate these findings in your next incentive program.

REWARDS PROGRAMS NOT MEETING EMPLOYEE NEEDS

Incentive programs can be great motivators, but they won't reach their potential if there's a mismatch between an organization's overall rewards program and what agents are looking for.

According to a Towers Perrin survey, *Engaging Employees for Enhanced Performance: A New Role and Direction for Total Rewards,* many employees say that their organizations are not delivering the kinds of rewards they want and need.

A sample of 1,500 employees identified the importance of certain reward elements and how well their employer was delivering those elements. Their responses indicated a significant gap.

Call center managers might want to work with their HR departments to determine the rewards elements considered highly important by call center agents, and their perception of how well those elements are being delivered.

COMPANY PROGRAM	CITED AS IMPORTANT BY EMPLOYEES	BEING MET TO GREAT EXTENT
Competitive Base Salary	84%	52%
Advancement Opportunities	72%	42%
Training Programs	72%	48%
Performance, Feedback, Coaching	71%	42%
Developmental Assignments	70%	47%
Variable Pay	69%	37%
Recognition Programs	53%	36%

Chapter 3

Inspired Agents Priceless

Motivated agents are priceless resources for call centers. In such a challenging and potentially monotonous job, agents need continuous inspiration, encouragement and recognition. Taking the 12 steps outlined here will help you to develop an incentive program that acknowledges call center agents' value and which motivates them to even higher levels of performance, contributes to overall organizational goals and enhances employee and customer satisfaction.

An Agent-Based Approach to Incentives
by Mark Haug

Let's face it—traditional call center incentive plans don't work. Whether you reward the few or build a "team" program to catch everyone, there are unintended consequences. Rewarding the few creates destructive competition, pitting winners against losers, breeding resentment. Move toward the team approach—to cast a wider net—and you have free-riders and malingerers, as well as a measurement that does not necessarily motivate and reward each individual.

Competition and incentive expert Alfie Kohn points out in his article "Why Incentive Plans Cannot Work" (*Harvard Business Review*) that the destructive competition in many incentive plans model the late economist Joseph Schumpeter's "creative destruction" in free enterprise—the ultimate obsolescence of that which is no longer competitive. Is this the message we want to send to our agents?

Developing an Incentive Plan

Incentives are more than rewards. Good incentive plans involve continuous and sustained motivation. Continuous and sustained motivation applied across all agents encourages individual productivity day-in and day-out. Where do you begin? The following case study serves as a warm-up exercise for developing an incentive plan.

COHO COLLECTIONS INC.

Coho is a privately held company responsible for collecting debts on all types of accounts. Its 93 call center collectors are assigned accounts based on several criteria. Collectors with the most seniority and who have met predetermined standards may choose which industries they handle. Those whose performance has slipped below standards are assigned industries based on their seniority and frequency of substandard performance.

About a year ago, management implemented an incentive program in the call center. They developed a recovery score that prioritizes accounts within each industry by its predicted value, regardless of how collectors are assigned to industries. The scoring system is based on historical data using a logit-loglinear model that predicts an unbiased estimate of the dollars collectable for a specific account. The scoring system allows management to "block" undesirable accounts from the queue and to prioritize accounts worthy of collection effort.

Call center collectors work eight-hour, staggered shifts, which are designed to achieve maximum coverage of times when debtors can be reached by phone. Unfortunately, the most "desirable" times are those with the lowest yield on collections.

The incentive plan rewards collectors on the dollars collected for any given calendar month. Payout is straightforward: the collector who collects the most gets the most. (The payout is in proportion to the dollars collected. For example, if four collectors—40 percent of 10 collectors—achieved $40, $30, $20 and $10, then the first would receive 40 percent of the monthly award money, the second collector would receive 30 percent, and so forth.) The top 40 percent of

---

COHO COLLECTIONS INCENTIVE PLANNING QUESTIONS

1. What are the advantages and disadvantages of predetermined standards?

2. What are the advantages and disadvantages of permitting seniority to determine where accounts are worked?

3. Should the decision rights to choose which industries to handle vest in management or the collectors?

4. Should the decision rights to choose which accounts to handle vest in management or the collectors?

5. Is this incentive plan tailored toward collectors' interests, management's interests, or both? To what degree?

6. Is the competitive component of the incentive plan a strength or weakness? Why?

7. Could the payout delay be improved? How?

8. Some collectors have been complaining that they never get any of the awards. Is this management's problem or their own problem?

---

collectors receive a payout according to their performance. Each collector must maintain an adequate quality score, which consists of two or more conversations each month that are randomly recorded and evaluated. Payout occurs at mid-month following the month of performance. The delay is due to the collections process: Once the collector secures a promise to pay the debt, some time will elapse (10-14 days on average) before the actual money is received, if it is received at all.

Incentive Planning Questions and Considerations

What can you learn from the Coho Collections incentive program? Although the context is specific to collections, Questions 1-8 (see the box on the facing page) are important considerations for most call center incentive plans. The first four questions go a long way toward determining the call center's culture. Although the answers will vary from center to center, it is important to define these parameters with clarity and execute accordingly. Failure to do so will result in excessive costs and a diminishing organizational effectiveness.

The answer to Question 5 requires a healthy dose of humility. Managers insist that their plans are tailored toward agents' interests: A reward is a good thing, a thing that agents want. They add that their team rewards build teams and that the corporate rewards get the agents excited about the company. Do you think your agents really care about your company? Unlikely. They are self-interested like everyone else all the way to the top. Sound corporate culture produces team players who balance self-interests with corporate interests by tying real individual interests to organizational performance. Security, acknowledgement, fair compensation are real agent interests. A good incentive plan speaks to these things when any agent performs in a way consistent with the corporate goals.

Question 6 addresses competition. On its face, competition is the struggle between adversaries—there is a desire to retain trade secrets, training regimens or whatever else facilitates success. Competition is great for discerning and improving the best, but it cannot bring everyone along. Schumpeter's creative

Chapter 3

destruction in the call center assures low morale and high attrition among the "losers."

Question 7 treats the important question of payout timing. Self-imposed constraints often force management to delay payout for two reasons: confirmation and convenience. Confirmation is the realistic need to confirm that, whatever activity has been recorded will be met with actual results. Convenience concerns are that more frequent payouts invite excessive administrative costs. Most managers, however, would pay out more frequently—indeed, daily—without these constraints.

Question 8 sharpens the focus for all managers who face an apparent contradiction: Although an agent adds value, management withholds rewards because the agent is not as good as the next agent. Should the agent "step up" or should management find some way to reward, even if only nominally, the valued agent when that agent has a great day or sustained improvement?

An Alternative Incentive Plan: Creative Construction

Many of the questions presented arise from a command-and-control mode of management that produces unnecessary constraints. Borrowing tools from Six Sigma and other disciplines, we can transform the command-and-control reward system into an agent-based incentive plan. In other words, we can evolve from "creative destruction" to "creative construction."

Whether an inbound or outbound call center, each agent is an individual business center: a franchise supported by the manager-franchiser. Management's role is to enable each franchise to succeed by providing adequate support. The agent's success results from whatever additional competence or abilities he brings beyond management's support. In keeping with this model,

- Franchisees do not compete against each other,
- The franchisee and franchiser have similar goals in that they depend on each other for their success,
- The franchisee has its own interests, which when satisfied, produces a more powerful franchiser.

To achieve this model, each agent is measured according to his own "scorecard." The scorecard provides real-time feedback of individual daily performance on several significant metrics. Each day, the agent's results are reported on a runs-chart indicating the agent's productivity for that day relative to the agent's past performances, averages and benchmarks. Production values that exceed a threshold are met with a nominal reward at the end of the day. Consistent and sustained production above average on any metric is also met with nominal rewards at the end of the day. Sustained and statistically significant improvement for the month is met with significantly higher rewards.

Beyond a period of time, depending on the industry, high achievers will reach their "max" and find this plan unsatisfying. A good retention and pay differential policy, however, will adequately address these agents so that their contributions are acknowledged and compensated for.

Significant evidence supports this franchiser-franchisee model, which reflects an agent-based approach to incentives. Factual, timely feedback sustains each and every agent's motivation on a daily basis, encourages camaraderie among agents, and frees up managerial time due to the automated nature of the fact-based feedback loop.

Chapter 3

A Look at What Works
in Agent Rewards and Recognition
by Greg Levin

No single tactic can assure that a call center will achieve low levels of burnout and turnover. However, the absence of *one* tactic—a strategic rewards and recognition program—can assure that a call center will *not* achieve those goals.

While high retention and performance rates rely on a number of factors and practices—e.g., focused recruiting/hiring, a competitive salary, effective training, opportunities for advancement—call center experts agree that those efforts will be wasted if agents don't feel that they are valued and appreciated on a regular basis.

"The money spent on recruitment, the time to interview, and training time can cost upward of $10,000 by the time you're done," says Kim Vey of Right on Queue, a consulting firm based in Innsifil in Ontario, Canada. "You can't afford to waste that investment by not paying close attention to [employee recognition and motivation] in your call center. ...Reward and recognition are the key elements required to achieve a good retention rate."

Such sentiments are echoed by Susan Heathfield, an independent management consultant specializing in human resource-related issues and opportunities. "Prioritize recognition for people, and you can ensure a positive, productive and innovative organizational climate. People who feel appreciated are more positive about themselves and their ability to contribute... and are potentially your best employees."

Heathfield adds that, while most managers believe that employee recognition and incentives are important, many don't put that belief into practice, or do so poorly.

"In my experience, recognition is scarce because of a combination of factors," she explains. "Time is an often-stated reason and, admittedly, recognition does take time. Another reason is that [some managers] don't know how to provide it effectively, so they have bad experiences when they do." She says that many

Chapter 3

105

assume "one size fits all" when they provide recognition and rewards, or use a "scatter approach" where they "put a lot out there and hope that some efforts will stick and create the results they want."

The Key Ingredients

Of course, not all call centers have failed in the recognition arena. Many have implemented strategic, well-rounded programs—programs that result in happier and, importantly, higher-performing agents whose commitment and effort help strengthen valuable customer relationships.

These programs, while varying significantly in the fine details, share certain common attributes that have contributed to their success. Here's a look at the key ingredients that top call centers have mixed into their agent rewards/recognition efforts:

• **The program features a healthy blend of both individual and team recognition.** Successful call centers have found that rewarding the few *and* the many is the best way to improve staff morale and retention centerwide. These centers have implemented not only "top achiever" awards that recognize strong performances by individual agents, but also team-based awards that help to foster camaraderie and common objectives among large groups of agents. For instance, at Boston Coach—an executive sedan service—agents earn points (which can later be converted to cash) not only for things like individual attendance and adherence to schedule, but also for improvements in the number of service failures for the center as a whole.

The more blending of individual and team awards, the better, according to Leslie Hansen Harps, a business writer and author of *Motivating Customer Service Employees.* "All-individual programs—which single out one or a handful of winners—can result in excessive competition among agents that can be harmful in a team setting," says Harps. "On the other hand, all-team programs—where everyone's contribution is recognized—may demotivate high performers who may feel their individual accomplishments are not appreciated."

• **Rewards and recognition are based on strategic productivity and qual-**

ity objectives. Successful call centers avoid the "numbers" trap when implementing and maintaining a rewards/recognition program. While straight productivity metrics such as talk time, calls per hour, and number of sales made often play a part in these center's programs, they are not the be-all and end-all in determining who (or what team) receives recognition. Top centers have effectively worked strategic quality metrics into the rewards and recognition mix as well, thus ensuring that agents focus on providing both efficient and effective service. For example, Independence Blue Cross (IBC) in Philadelphia not only considers productivity metrics such as staff time and after-call work when rewarding agents, it also places a heavy emphasis on such areas as accuracy, professionalism, attendance and punctuality.

Disregard quality metrics in your recognition program, and your center is doomed, says Harps. "If you are committed to delivering top-notch service, your incentive programs must include a balance of quality and quantity components. Over-emphasizing 'the numbers'—i.e., number of calls handled per shift—can negatively affect quality and service."

In addition to giving quality the attention it deserves, some call centers are starting to do away with those productivity metrics over which agents have little or no control. IBC, for example has removed the "average talk time" statistic from its reward and recognition program. Companies like Boston Coach and many others have done the same with their "number of calls handled per shift" metric.

• **The program features a mixture of monetary and non-monetary rewards.** "Just give me money" may be what John, Paul, George and Ringo were shouting, but it appears that agents are singing a slightly different tune. Numerous studies—including one by the American Management Association— have revealed that, while call center staff certainly appreciate cash rewards, they may be more motivated by non-monetary ones. Many centers have heeded such study findings—as well as their own agents' suggestions—and implemented rewards/recognition programs that feature both financial gifts as well as things like paid days off, gift certificates, merchandise, achievement awards and luncheons.

Chapter 3

According to American Express Incentive Services (www.aeis.com), "When companies try to motivate employees with an extra paycheck, the award dollars typically go toward the necessities: laundry detergent, diapers, car payments. But non-cash awards… leave participants with tangible reminders or fond memories of their hard work." AEIS cites a three-to-one return on investment in non-cash rewards compared to cash rewards.

• **Agents themselves actively participate in the maintenance of the program.** Of course, the best way to know what will best motivate agents on the job and earn their gratitude is simply to ask them. The vast majority of call centers with effective rewards/recognition programs in place regularly seek feedback from their staff to cull new ideas and to ensure that agents are satisfied with how the program is being run. This is typically done via surveys and/or discussions during team meetings. However, some call centers have started giving staff more control—creating agent-led incentives task forces/committees that empower members with substantial planning and decision-making authority. At Mountain America Credit Union in Salt Lake City, Utah, for example, a Morale Team develops and implements events and activities intended to inject fun into the atmosphere while keeping fellow agents focused on customer service goals.

AmeriCredit Corp. has a similar agent-led team in place to help recognize staff contributions and to boost morale and performance. The Special Activities Committee meets monthly to plan events and contests, most of which feature food and gift certificates as prizes. In addition, the center has a Team Recognition program in place, where each team is allotted $50 per month and is given the power to decide which team member or members deserve to be rewarded.

• **The program values employee diversity.** Call centers today feature very eclectic employee bases, with agents ranging in age from 18 to over 70. Differences in race, cultural and educational background, religion and general interests are also common among agent colleagues. The most successful call centers have learned the importance of factoring such employee diversity into their rewards and recognition programs.

"We have people who have worked here for 20 years, and their incentive needs are different from [those of] an agent who is 24 years old. You have to consider the differences and needs of individuals," says Charlotte Baptie, field market service manager for Gordon Food Service in Ontario, Canada. To ensure that no agents feel alienated by the center's rewards/recognition practices, Baptie strives to keep the programs varied and fresh—implementing a wide range of small monthly awards, prizes and recognition efforts rather than focusing on a couple of big contests.

At JP Morgan Chase and Co. Cardmember Services, agent diversity isn't only taken into consideration when planning incentives, it is the very basis of the company's most important employee recognition effort. Each year, the company's four call centers (Tampa, Fla.; San Antonio, Texas; Tempe, Ariz.; and Hicksville, N.Y.) pay homage to the rich diversity of their staff via a series of eight separate month-long celebrations: Black History Month, Women's History Month, Disability Awareness Month, Gay/Lesbian Pride Month, Asian-Pacific Heritage Month, Hispanic Heritage Month, Multicultural Month, and Native American Heritage Month. Each center features its own diversity steering committee that organizes each month's activities, which include cultural awareness discussions led by guest speakers, as well as musical and dance performances by professional groups.

Keep the Circle Spinning

Of course, not all call centers have the budget for such extensive celebrations. The good news is that they don't have to for their rewards and recognition programs to work. Many managers have learned to be creative in stretching tight budgets to ensure that staff stay inspired and feel appreciated. Gordon Food Service's Baptie, for instance, often rewards deserving agents with food certificates and merchandise that has been donated by corporate sponsors. Another simple, cost-effective and popular approach Baptie frequently employs is to post kudos on office bulletin boards whenever an individual or team of agents goes beyond the call of duty. As she explains, "Even the smallest recognition is important."

Chapter 3

Consultant Heathfield agrees, adding that companies that are lazy in terms of their rewards and recognition efforts risk losing not only agents, but customers as well.

"Make recognition a common practice—not a scarce resource—in your organization. ...Motivated employees do a better job of serving customers well. Happy customers buy more products and are committed to use your services. More customers buying more increases your profitability and success. It's an endless circle; hop on the employee recognition bandwagon to keep the circle spinning."

JUST A SAMPLE

There is no limit to the ways in which call centers can recognize valued staff. Below is a list of just some of the many rewards/recognition ideas that have been used by successful call centers worldwide:

- Agents' contributions cited in company newsletter or on the intranet
- Public praise at team or centerwide meetings
- Lunch/dinner for top performers
- Agent(s) sent to a conference, seminar or workshop of their choice
- Agent(s) represent the call center at an interdepartmental meeting
- Agent(s) given the opportunity to work on special off-phone projects
- Gift certificates to local stores
- A "performance points" system that enables agents to redeem points for cash, prizes or paid time off
- Plaques or framed certificates of achievement
- Tickets to movies, concerts, sporting events, etc.
- All-expense-paid weekend away at a local resort
- A day at a spa
- "Agent Appreciation Week" celebrations
- An annual awards dinner
- Increased opportunities for empowerment and self-management
- Names/photos of consistently high performing agents placed on the call center's "Wall of Fame"
- Handwritten "thank you" notes

The Benefits of Online Incentive Programs
by Chris Heide

A well-designed agent incentive program can work wonders in a call center by improving agent productivity, boosting morale and reducing turnover. But the key to making these programs work lies in the ability to track agent performance accurately and reward desired behaviors quickly.

Program administration is where traditional incentive programs often falter. Keeping participants apprised of their standings by informing them of how many points they've earned, how close they are to achieving a reward and how their current performance compares to other participants is essential for several reasons:

- Informing participants of their progress helps keep them committed to the program.
- Companies can gauge the incentive program's effectiveness, which allows managers to fine-tune it while it's in progress.
- It's the vehicle by which information is captured for timely reports and analysis.

Without careful administration, even the most well-designed incentive program will suffer.

Drawbacks of Paper-Based Incentive Programs

Here's a case in point: A California credit union has several ongoing call center incentive programs. Payouts for incentives, which are based on referrals, are tracked manually. The process has led to reporting errors, slow payout of incentives and disputes between agents about who should qualify for a particular incentive. For example, the credit union pays agents $3 per car sales referral, even if the customer doesn't qualify for the loan or decides not to buy a new car. Agents receive $8 for a referral that turns into a sale.

While the program may sound pretty straightforward, there are potential drawbacks. Because the referrals are tracked on paper, there is a significant lag

Chapter 3

between the time when the desired behavior is performed and when it is rewarded. In addition, Customer A may talk with one agent one week and another the next—but both agents refer the customer for a car loan. Paper-based programs make it more difficult to track double-referrals.

Benefits of Online Incentive Programs

Over the past few years, many companies have eliminated the paper-based obstacles by moving their incentive programs online.

"The Internet offers the means to deliver communications, training, measurement and rewards as never before imagined—and draw them together for unparalleled synergy," says Bill Termini of Hinda Incentives, a Chicago-based incentive house.

The critical difference between a traditional program and the online alternative is the speed at which participants send and receive information. Tapping into the Internet gives your program a sense of immediacy.

Although companies have been experimenting with online incentive programs for the past few years, the real power the Internet can bring to incentive programs is just being discovered, says Mike Hadlow, president of USMotivation, an Atlanta-based provider of both online and off-line incentive programs. He adds that recent advances in technology have made online programs more user-friendly. For example:

• **Programs are customizable.** Tailored reward catalogs are available. In addition, it's fairly easy to create incentive themes around recurring holidays and special events, such as Customer Service Week, Thanksgiving and Christmas.

• **Data management is more flexible.** New systems allow for multiple query levels of performance data. Since data can be reported by region, agent and product line, managers can identify areas for additional training, which can be supplied online and customized to the individual.

• **Reporting systems are more robust and flexible.** Companies can take advantage of more graphics to make reporting more user-friendly. In addition, user-defined reports instead of pre-programmed reports are possible.

- **Program administration is simple.** Making changes, reporting results and mining data are relatively simple tasks. All the information that program participants need can be sent, received and viewed on a real-time basis. Email programs also allow administrators to get an idea of participants' interest in a specific program by tracking their email behavior, such as whether they open a message or just delete it. (Although this capability exists, Hadlow says tracking employee participation is better measured through incentive program performance and results.)

- **Achievement can be quickly rewarded.** Agents participating in online incentive programs can log onto the Web site anytime to check their personal status, including goals met and points earned. They can also browse digital catalogs and instantly order a wide range of merchandise and other awards.

- **Online programs build a greater sense of community.** Password-protected Web sites allow participants to enter chat rooms and access bulletin boards to discuss the program with other agents. Some companies even post pictures of high-performing participants online, along with brief write-ups about them.

- **Higher participation.** The speed of redemption, as well as instant communication and regular tracking of results, appeals to people and encourages them to participate.

- **Lower costs.** "By utilizing Internet technology, we have seen most of our clients' administrative expenses reduced to 5 percent or less of their total program budget, compared to 15 to 25 percent in a traditional program," says Hinda's Termini. "Many companies take the savings and spend them on more valuable awards, which often helps to encourage greater participation."

Even more significant savings are realized through efficient administration. "Research indicates that the cost of processing a single transaction through a paper catalog and phone-in order is about $15, compared to $1 through an online tool," he says.

Chapter 3

Fun Should Be a Key Component

Whether your incentive programs are online or off-line, making them fun will boost participation, says Bob Nelson, president and founder of Nelson Motivation Inc., a management training consulting company located in San Diego, Calif. "There's a big difference between getting people to come to work and getting them to do their best work," he says. "Making work fun brings out the best in people."

Tyler Mitchell, vice president of product development at Snowfly, an online incentive firm based in Laramie, Wyo., agrees that fun should be a critical component of any online incentive program. Snowfly's online approach is to link improved employee behavior to the incentive itself, and make the reporting procedure more enjoyable by making it a game. For instance, the utilities division of a credit processing firm implemented an online incentive program in its Dallas call center. Each position has set job performance requirements that are measured on a daily, weekly or monthly basis. Snowfly's Web-based program's user interface is a graphic of a slot machine. Agents who reach their job performance goals earn daily "pulls" on the slot machine.

To ensure agents aren't playing the virtual slot machine when they're supposed to be taking calls, they must log onto the program from special kiosks in the call center or from their home computers. Each time they play, points are deposited into the agents' personal accounts. Points are accumulated and can be redeemed online for various rewards, including gift certificates, merchandise and scheduled time off.

The call center's agents are enthusiastic about the program, says one supervisor. Agent performance and morale is up, which is reflected in the quality of service provided to callers.

"One of the best features is the ability for supervisors and managers to provide immediate feedback and recognition to agents," adds one manager. "Supervisors receive information about their agents' daily performance and have the opportunity to send an immediate message to congratulate them."

ONLINE INCENTIVE PROGRAM RESOURCES

Following is a brief listing of organizations that can help to design an online incentive program or move your existing program to the Internet:

- All Star Incentive Marketing (www.incentiveusa.com)
- Bravanta (www.bravanta.com)
- CompanyDNA (www.companydna.com)
- Diamond H Recognition (www.diamondh.com)
- eMaritz Inc. (www.emaritz.com)
- Galactic Ltd. (www.galacticmarketing.com)
- Hinda Incentives (www.hinda.com)
- InMarketing Group (www.inmarketinggroup.com)
- Paramax (www.pmx.com)
- SalesDriver.com (www.salesdriver.com)
- Snowfly (www.Snowfly.com)
- The Sharper Image (www.sharperimage.com)
- USMotivation (www.usmotivation.com)
- Xceleration (www.xceleration.com)

ASSOCIATIONS

- The Incentive Promotion Council (www.incentivecentral.org) was formed to protect the rights of organizations to motivate customers and employees through the intelligent and ethical use of incentive programs. Made up of the leading associations and trade shows in the incentive field and some of the top suppliers, the federation monitors federal regulations that could affect the proper use of incentive programs. It also manages the Incentive Promotion Campaign, an industrywide effort to promote professional use of incentives.

- Incentive Marketing Association (IMA) (www.incentivemarketing.org) represents members who provide incentive merchandise and services. It offers incentive seminars in conjunction with The Motivation Show in Chicago and the New York Premium Incentive Marketplace. It also sponsors the Online Incentive Council, (www.useonlineincentives.org) a strategic industry group whose member companies promote the benefits of online incentive solutions.

Chapter 3

Chapter 4: Agent Development

Few things motivate employees more than viable opportunities to expand their skills and grow in their careers. In numerous studies, agents have labeled "professional development" as a prime reason for committing to an organization. In many call centers, skills-based pay initiatives are replacing the traditional vertical promotion approach to career development. In fact, there are many proven practices call centers can adopt—regardless of the size of the center or organization—to ensure that agents have room to grow and opportunities to grab on their way to becoming seasoned call center professionals.

Effective Career Progression Programs Balance Both Staff and Business Needs

by Susan Hash

The competition for skilled agents shows no signs of relenting. The increase in call center openings, available contact channels and types of agent skills required make it a job-seeker's market—and the outlook is pretty grim for call centers that don't have some type of agent development and retention process in place.

The historical corporate ladder approach to staff development has never been a viable option for call centers. After all, there are a finite number of supervisory and management positions available.

Instead, a more effective staff-development approach is to prepare agents for the future of your business by taking into consideration individual staff needs and company goals. You'll also find that it's easier to get executive-level support and funding for call center career programs if they're aligned with overall business needs.

Depending on the type of advancement opportunities available in your organization and your call center requirements, most centers follow one of two basic approaches to agent development. One focuses on an individualized acquisition of skill sets, while the other involves more structured tracks or levels through which agents can progress.

Identify the Skills Your Company Finds Desirable

AT&T's Consumer Services call centers (which include some 30 various-sized call centers nationwide) has created a career development program for its customer care reps called the Associate-to-Management Advancement Program (AMAP). It addresses two specific business needs that surfaced a few years ago:

• Local call centers recognized the need for a more disciplined approach to career progression (specifically, from the non-management account rep positions into management and supervisory positions), which would be perceived as

Chapter 4

objective by account reps.

• AT&T wanted its management, organizationwide, to have consistent leadership skills. It developed a management-leadership framework, which consists of 10 competencies identified as the core leadership skills required for AT&T managers.

The call centers' AMAP process was designed with this framework in mind. "We wanted the people who were being promoted or hired into our call center management positions to have demonstrated the relevant competencies in this

DIFFERENTIATE BETWEEN SERVICE AND MANAGEMENT SKILLS

When developing a career-progression model, it's important to consider a path for agents who are not management- or career-oriented. "The reality is that there are some agents who are not interested in promotion, or who might not be viewed as potential candidates for promotion," says Jerard Kehoe, AT&T sourcing and selection director. "Success as a customer care rep does not necessarily predict success as a supervisor. The decision about how to develop reps into supervisors and which ones to select for promotion should be based on the skills that are relevant to supervision."

At Unum Provident Insurance, for instance, managers found that clear differentiators existed between being a senior-level rep and a specialist, says Anne O'Neil, call center director. For instance, some specific abilities identified were:

• Change management
• Problem identification and resolution
• Interaction with peers
• Conflict resolution
• Group leadership abilities.

To develop agents displaying management-type skills, the Unum Provident call centers created Mentor and Leadership Certification tracks in its career-progression model, with "distinct definitions of the behavior we're looking for and the competencies," O'Neil says. Agent progression in these areas is measured through 360-degree feedback and management observation.

new management leadership framework," says Jerard Kehoe, sourcing and selection director for AT&T.

Skills-Based Development Relies on Individual Assessment

AT&T's AMAP essentially works as a skills-acquisition process in which agents can learn new skills at their own pace. At the same time, all of AMAP's phases are based on the management-leadership framework and target several of the skills outlined in it, such as planning and organizing, implementing with excellence and continuous learning.

In fact, as an individual moves up the AT&T management ladder, his or her performance continues to be appraised on that same framework, says Kehoe. "We've integrated AMAP with the other HR levers and strategies that represent the way AT&T wants to develop its managers—that's one of the program's strengths."

Candidates for the program are identified by the local supervisors who have the responsibility of coaching agents, not only for on-the-job performance, but also with an eye toward developing skills for eventual promotion.

The first stage of AMAP is called "Readiness Assessment." Supervisors assess agents' readiness to enter into the AMAP process based on their own judgment and the agent's past work behavior. The supervisor's evaluation also needs to be confirmed by the call center's local human resources manager.

After an agent is identified as being ready, he or she can participate in the next cycle of skills-assessment procedures, which are scheduled at each center two or three times a year.

Skill Paths Should Be Flexible
to Meet Changing Caller Needs

Another company that has taken the skills-development approach to agent growth is Earthlink. The organization recently completed a merger with MindSpring Enterprises to create the second-largest Internet service provider in the United States with seven technical support call centers, which range from

150 to 500 agents.

Director of technical support Mark Hinkle describes Earthlink's skills-development process as similar to getting a college degree. Agents can take various classes; once they pass, they move on to the next course. While there is a slight hierarchy in the order of skills, the path is pretty varied depending on the agent's personal goals and customer needs.

An important component of Earthlink's agent development program is the flexibility to react to changing customer demands, says Hinkle.

For instance, recently, the technical support organization expanded its agents' skills to focus on the Macintosh platform. "When the Apple iMac came out, the demand for Macintosh technical support just went through the ceiling," says Hinkle. "We've expanded the ability of our reps to take those calls. If we'd stayed with any kind of rigid hierarchy, we would be doing a disservice to our customers."

Group Skill Sets to Create a More Structured Career Path

A more structured approach to agent development calls for outlining specific levels or scales of progression and identifying the specific skill sets contained in each level.

While that seems like an overwhelming task "if you dig deep, you can find them," says Kim Weakley, assistant vice president and national call center manager at World Savings and Loan in San Antonio, Texas.

"But for the call centers that use skills-based routing, it becomes even easier. That's a very clear-cut way to build a career-progression model that will allow agents to grow," Weakley says.

In her call center, there are nine progression levels in the scale—three overall position levels and three sub-levels within each. For instance, Basic I, II and III Reps; Advanced I, II and III Reps; and Expert I, II and III Reps.

All new-hires are considered Basic I Reps. They're given an initial eight-week training program in products, systems and customer service skills, as well as an overview of call center statistics "to understand the information we're going to be feeding back to them," she says.

After the first 90 days, new agents' skill levels are evaluated. At that point, most have reached the Basic III Rep level and they can sign up for the skills-assessment testing, which is conducted once a month.

Agents are individually coached by supervisors on the specific skills they need to progress to the next level. The call center also has an in-house team of trainers who work with agents on technical skills.

Unum Provident Insurance has developed a similar career path for staff at its centers. "We've created a trainee position for entry-level reps, plus a Rep I, Rep II and Specialists jobs," explains call center director Anne O'Neil.

Within each rep job there are three tracks, each of which contains different skill sets based on various products. And the Specialist position contains three separate career paths agents can select:

1. Super reps are customer-focused agents who truly enjoy working in the call center on the phone dealing with customers. They generally want to acquire more product and systems knowledge, but aren't really interested in managing others. This path allows them to become subject-matter experts, cross-train on products and act as mentors for newer agents.

2. Training/quality/technology experts are trained to offer immediate internal support for the call center. "Even though we have support areas within IT, it's beneficial to have people on staff with the ability to respond to technology issues quickly," says O'Neil. "They can often look at a situation with a system and get our people back on track within minutes vs. having to call something in and wait."

3. A leadership path is available for management-oriented agents. "We give them opportunities to participate in reviews, act as backup for management, attend meetings in place of managers and conduct call observations," she says.

Develop an Objective Assessment Process

One of the most critical aspects of an agent development program is an assessment process that's viewed by participants as fair and unbiased.

Chapter 4

Kehoe feels that AT&T's AMAP assessment procedures make it distinct in that area. "It has formalized steps to objectively assess the skill levels the account reps have developed," he says. That process includes three events:

1. A written test that measures problem-solving and information-processing skills;

2. An "in-basket exercise" in which agents simulate being a manager by handling problem situations in a virtual in-basket; and

3. A discussion with a panel of trained interviewers who rate agents based on a pre-defined set of criteria.

While testing procedures need to be consistently applied to avoid any appearance of favoritism, it's also important to know your agents, says World Savings' Weakley.

At her call center, agents go to a "test region" off the call center floor to process five to 10 customer requests, which can range from customer address changes to more complicated, sensitive issues like fixing checks that have been encoded incorrectly.

An unanticipated discovery with this process, however, was that some agents have "test phobia," she says. "They may be extremely proficient at performing certain types of tasks or calls on the floor, but when they know they're doing their monthly skills assessment, they freak out."

Weakley has worked around certain agents' test anxiety by using "sneak attacks." "We may give them something that needs to be done, and we don't tell them it's a skills assessment," she explains. The only potential hazard was that agents would be handling test issues live on the system, she points out, but adds that "we make sure we check it the same day, so we can delete those transactions and not impact the customer."

Extend Growth Possibilities Beyond the Call Center

If your agent development program is limited to your call center, at some point, you may find that you have a staff of highly trained experts—with no place else to go.

While the AT&T AMAP process is specifically focused on the progression from customer care rep to the entry-level call center supervisory position, agents

---

ALIGNING AGENT PROGRAMS ACROSS CULTURES AND CENTERS

Mergers and acquisitions have a definite impact on agent-development programs in terms of growth potential, skills involved, job descriptions, promotional opportunities and the consistency of assessment. Trying to integrate two (or more) distinct points of view on staff development can be trying for managers when different cultures, customers and procedures are involved.

Last year, after Unum and Provident merged to create Unum Provident Insurance, managers were tasked with creating one agent-development program for the company's three call centers, located in Chattanooga, Tenn., Columbia, S.C.; and Portland, Maine, each of which served different types of customers.

At an initial planning meeting, which included representatives from each site, each manager detailed the programs currently in place at their centers. "We were trying to determine what would make sense [for all three centers]," says Anne O'Neil, Unum Provident Insurance call center director. "It really came together based on what we heard from the agents in terms of their needs, and also what we, as the management team, felt we could manage. Each site had something that was a little different which we could leverage—and we took the best practices of each site."

The model was tested at the Portland call center to make sure it would work effectively and to give managers a chance to make adjustments. Next, O'Neil presented the model to an internal "roles group," which acts as a sounding board for programs developed around call center jobs, for more feedback and to identify any gaps in skills or job families. The final test was a review by the Human Resources department.

Eventually, O'Neil says, the goal is to bring other related areas under the same umbrella, such as a customer claims call center, employment call center, sales support center and a broker commissions group.

Chapter 4

who become qualified for entry-level management positions via the AMAP process can go into any number of positions that involve entry-level management within AT&T, says Kehoe. In fact, the organization has an internal post-and-bid staffing process that allows customer care reps to scan a staffing system for vacancies outside the call center in which they might be interested.

Earthlink's company culture also follows a promote-from-within philosophy, says Hinkle. In fact, he adds, "the majority of our company is staffed out of our call center. There are a lot of folks in executive-level positions who started out on the phones, including myself."

Typically, he says, agents move into areas like network operations, engineering, telecommunications and the MIS department.

Call center managers at Earthlink make a point of helping individual agents to progress, and take into consideration any skills or interests agents have—even those not used in the call center. For instance, if an agent has an interest in Web design, their supervisor may give them a non-phone project to help showcase their skills for the company's Web Design Group.

Related company areas offer another avenue to boost agent growth. World Savings' call center extends agent learning through cross-training with its tax and insurance call center groups. It's a win-win for both areas, says Weakley. Her center trains reps from the tax and insurance groups to take calls when the volume gets heavy. At the same time, her agents cross-train on tax and insurance functions for those times when the tax group gets backed up. "Once we complete this, we're going to roll out a new skill level called a Universal Agent," she says.

Compensate Agents for Growth

Naturally, you can't expect agents to be motivated to learn and grow if there is no compensation for their efforts. Unless, of course, they're planning to take those skills elsewhere, which undermines your program's fundamental goal.

Agents at Unum Provident Insurance are assessed and certified for learning the skills included in their job-level tracks. After they've successfully demonstrated those skills on the job for six months, they receive a pay increase.

Because the program was just recently implemented, it's currently being self-funded with call center budget dollars. But, O'Neil says, since agent salaries were "not that far from where they needed to be, it's not a huge hit." However, she adds, based on the progression tracks that have been set up and the potential for retaining more experienced staff over the long term, her company's HR and finance managers have indicated that the future increases in compensation for agents are not unreasonable.

At World Savings, there are team and individual bonus opportunities associated with skills development. Pay-for-performance bonuses are paid quarterly to teams that reach pre-set expectations. Some goals are centerwide, such as service level objectives, while others focus on team projects and the skill level of team members. So, for instance, to get the team bonus, all members must be able to test at a certain skill level, such as Advanced I Rep.

Bonus opportunities for individual agents increase with each level, as well as for working less-desired shifts.

Here's how it works: An Advanced I Rep can receive a bonus of up to 2.1 percent of his or her salary; an Expert 3 can receive almost 5 percent. "There's quite a jump in compensation, and it's incrementally staged going up the scale," says Weakley.

Also, in each of the categories, there is an A, B and C designation for shifts. For example, A is the 8 a.m. to 5 p.m. shift (highly desirable); B is 9 a.m. to 6 p.m.; and C is 10 a.m. to 7 p.m. (the least preferred shift). "We pay higher bonuses for C shifts," Weakley says.

"We try to cover all angles so that we can keep people on the less-preferred shifts, and there's an incentive to learn more on their own, be able to handle more tasks and create a greater repertoire of skills," she explains. "But we also want them to cover for each other—so if you have somebody who's a little bit slower at developing skills on your team, you're not going to bash them, you're going to help them. And it really has worked out well."

Chapter 4

Do Agent Development Programs Impact Retention?

Absolutely, says Weakley. In 1998, her call center's turnover rate was between 55 to 60 percent. "We had a churning," she says. "We'd get them in and train them. They'd stay for six months and then they'd leave. We've dropped that rate to 17 percent."

AT&T is in the process of developing a plan to evaluate the effectiveness of the AMAP process, which has been in place for about two years. Kehoe points out that, based on employee satisfaction surveys, agents feel more positive about their progression opportunities. In addition, he says, "the early indications are that the people who are promoted via AMAP are demonstrating success in those management positions." Currently, about 670 customer care reps have started the testing portion of the program. And of those, about 56 percent have successfully completed testing and have become qualified for promotion.

The effort of setting up a program is well worth it, says O'Neil. "Don't be afraid of negative thinking in the beginning, or of anything in your current environment that tells you it won't work," she says. "Just open up your thinking and be willing to explore all possibilities."

Elements of a Successful Agent Development Program

by Anne Nickerson

> *"Career development… can be said to be at the core of human resource development. It requires the integration of human resource planning, assessment, selection and places appraisal, training, development, performance and reward management within the organizational structure and culture."*
>
> *Marina Nordin*
> *"Career Development and Planning Strategy,"* New Strait Times

Do you wonder if implementing a career path in your call center or company will make a difference in your staff morale and retention? Are you convinced that putting a career path in place is right, but don't know where to begin? Should you certify your agent, supervisory and management staff? Are you wondering whether or not the benefits will be worth the time, effort and expense? If you're grappling with any of these questions, read on for some thoughts and solutions you should consider.

Will the Benefits Outweigh the Effort and Cost?

Many call center experts agree that the benefits do, in fact, far outweigh the efforts, resources and costs required to implement and maintain a career-path program. The result of a recent study by staffing services firm Manpower indicated that among the top motivators for call center personnel are the opportunities to learn new skills and to be offered continuous new challenges and support for personal growth.

And, as many managers can confirm, the more professionally you treat call center agents, the better they will treat their internal and external customers. Employees who are happy and satisfied with their jobs exude their confidence and satisfaction in the way that they approach and handle customers.

Chapter 4

129

Key Components of a Career Development Program

If you've already put individual agent performance plans and goals in place, implemented a quality assurance program and set up developmental coaching processes for your call center, then you've already made a strong start toward a career path program.

The next steps include identifying a progression of skills and measurements for increased complexity and job responsibility. Following are a few essential components for putting together your career path program.

First, identify the competencies, key skills, behaviors and attributes that are required for success on the job. One example may be "customer focus," which might include specific behaviors, such as the ability to:

- Identify caller needs;
- Acknowledge the impact of services and products (or lack thereof) on cus-

---

TIPS FOR CREATING A SUCCESSFUL CAREER PATH

Here are a few tips, suggestions and lessons learned from managers who have created effective career paths in their call centers.

- Create a project team consisting of human resource experts, agents and managers.

- Get buy-in to any changes you may make by inviting staff members representing each area of the call center to help design the program.

- Design, develop and implement quickly.

- Set and manage expectations.

- Create a formal and informal feedback process.

- Make adjustments quickly.

- Set up a mentoring program.

- Consider tuition reimbursement and local educational alliances.

- Determine policies regarding opportunities within and outside the department.

- Create a "marketing plan" to brand the image, and launch with "hoopla."

- Measure and publish results.

---

tomer satisfaction;

- Use appropriate probing techniques;
- Find solutions;
- Follow through on customer requests using available resources; and
- Demonstrate a courteous attitude.

Once your competency model is identified, create "job clusters." These are the specific job tasks in which the competencies are applied. They also become the foundation for your compensation planning.

Most career path options take a building-block approach where specific tasks need to be successfully accomplished in order to move from one level to the next. This often requires a well-thought-out pay and reward strategy where base pay increases drive skills acquisition, and some type of variable pay is linked to business results. In addition, create a strong reward and recognition program to continue to drive results—both individual and team—and to maintain a culture that values learning. At a minimum, a successful program should outline expectations and standards, as well as the specific steps necessary to advance.

Some call centers align skills development with agent certification programs, which offer a clear outline for setting expectations and goals for staff, as well as a succession plan for the organization.

Certification programs also act as a form of reward and recognition for agents. Typically, agents receive diplomas or documentation (and sometimes monetary rewards) indicating that they have not only learned new skills and behaviors, but can apply them and maintain high performance on the job.

Training and Feedback Options

Besides outlining the development process, don't overlook two of the most critical components of any career-path program: the availability of training and performance feedback processes.

Many call centers have been very creative at offering high-quality options while keeping training costs to a minimum. For instance, some viable alternatives include partnering with local community institutions and educational programs, obtaining funds from economic development programs, using in-house experts or contracting for vendor-supplied programs.

While some centers have the resources to offer one-on-one coaching and mentoring, others take advantage of staff input, as well. An effective feedback method is 360-degree assessment, in which peers, teammates and supervisors offer individuals feedback for an objective, well-rounded view of a their performance.

Generally, most call center managers find that offering career development options gives agents a feeling of control over their destiny, increases their passion for their work and energizes them with a sense of pride about their achievements and optimism about their future. Call centers that have implemented career development programs find that they experience lower turnover, attract and retain high performers, and maintain high morale.

Changing Agent Development Opportunities in the Multichannel Environment

by Wanda Sitzer

As customer touchpoints evolve from the simplicity of voice-only contact to the more complex email and Web-chat interactions, the call center industry must embrace more sophisticated profiling, training and management techniques.

Mundane tasks can be handled by self-service functions, leaving your agents free to develop relationships that require more involvement and skill than merely issuing templated responses.

We have to acknowledge the awesome responsibility today's agents have in shaping customers' experiences and delivering on companies' brand promises and service commitments in a multimedia environment.

The Elements of E-Skill Training

Employing agents proficient in "CyberSpeak" or "NetSpeak"–a language far different from the formal prose taught in high school language classes, and yet, not as informal as phone conversations encouraged in our contact centers–will differentiate the companies that thrive vs. those that only survive.

An e-skill set can be cultivated with your existing staff through practice and aptitude. However, practice does require time away from the phones (not just on-the-job training), which is a stretch for call centers, but not a luxury.

Reps need to practice electronic communication tasks, such as categorizing email and determining whether messages require templated responses or customization. Honing perceptivity to decipher customer needs and customer tone in a brief written message is no simple task. Add the element of speed for Web-chat sessions and online navigating, plus focus and concentration for handling multiple sessions–and everyone will agree that multichannel contact centers require a sophisticated combination of skills.

Chapter 4

Align Service Interactions with Company Image

In addition to proper grammar usage, agents need to be able to embrace language that jives with the soul of the organization. In too many companies, customer service has been homogenized to the point of "smile skills"—saying the company name at the beginning and end of the call, and using the customer's name at least once in the conversation.

Web interaction, phone interaction, packaging, direct marketing and awareness ads should all line up. If we live by the premise that says that customers want to do business with us, in part, because of how we've presented ourselves through marketing, then, indeed, they won't be turned off when we let a little of our essence into the quality exchange—rather they'll bask in it. It will confirm to our callers that we are who they thought we were, and that the company experience is what they imagined it would be.

Companies should consider more special ways of handling online and phone interactions rather than seeking a routine, consistent, generic manner. For instance, the title for help desk agents at www.techknow-how.com is "techknowledgist," which says it all. Or how about "egreetologist"? That's what agents at Egreetings are called. Titles like these make sense and change the tenor of the conversation—which agents can live up to with unique company brand training.

Multiple Channels and Skills Builds a Case for Higher Pay

Awarding commensurate salaries is essential if our reps are to succeed in elevating the call center image and cementing the brand relationship. Call centers can build a case at the CEO level that agents breathe life into the customer experience and bring a return on investment to executives' brand promises. This complex professional competency requires respect and an environment in which agents can feel the effects of their contributions—a leading job motivator.

The challenges for call centers are to design career paths, interaction institutions and creative settings that will attract high-quality candidates in a tight labor market, and nurture and retain our most valuable asset.

Chapter 4

Supervisor Development: Selecting the Right Agents to Grow

by Susan Hash

Promotions are an essential component of career paths and development programs. However, many times the best frontline agents don't make the best supervisors or team leaders, says Tom Langstone, owner/principal of TBK Consulting in Holbrook, Mass.

Managers often make the mistake of promoting top-performing agents as a form of recognition for a job well done. But "the person who can do the job well isn't necessarily the person who can lead others to do the job well," Langstone says.

Yet there are many great managers who started out as agents, and there are a few very definite advantages to promoting supervisors and team leaders from within the center.

For instance, a key benefit is that frontline agents already know the company and call center culture and will be able to carry on that culture, says Langstone.

"They know the organization's policies and procedures, whereas if you bring in someone from outside the company, it will take them at least six months to get up to speed—even if they have top supervisory or leadership skills. Also, there will be credibility issues (with existing staff), so it will take them awhile to fit in."

Managers agree. Agents at American Express Financial Services' two Mutual Fund and Certificate Transactions call centers develop strong technical knowledge of the system, company culture and procedures, says Director Shirley Shimota. That foundation provides a great advantage to both individuals and the company by reducing training time, she says.

That's true, according to Customer Sales and Service Team Leader Jamie Weinhardt at the *London Free Press* in Ontario, Canada. Weinhardt, who has been a team leader for about six years, started out as a customer sales and service rep-

A FOUR-STEP PROCESS FOR SUPERVISOR TRAINING/SUPPORT

You can use your frontline agent training process as a model to build a comprehensive training program for new supervisors and team leaders. There are four steps recommended to ensure the success of the new supervisor:

ORIENTATION

New supervisors should be given some kind of introduction to the position. This can be formatted in different ways, but the main objective is to clearly identify the roles and responsibilities of the frontline supervisor. Human resources personnel and upper management can help to offer the right perspective for orientation.

TRAINING

The actual training process for supervisors should be conducted using a variety of methods (e.g., classroom, seminars, self-paced, mentors, e-learning, etc.). The focus of the training should be to identify knowledge and skill areas that are outside of the frontline agents' knowledge and skill set, such as leadership, decision making, conflict management, coaching, etc. Training in these areas is usually done by human resource professionals, training staff members, call center managers or experienced supervisors. The best supervisor training programs also include situational role playing. This gives the trainee a chance to use new knowledge and skills in a realistic, but simulated environment.

NESTING/SHADOWING

Many call centers find that providing new supervisors with a "nesting" opportunity by having the person shadow or "co-manage" a team for a period of time can help to ensure the individual's success as a leader. Nesting gives new supervisors a chance to observe an experienced supervisor's work flow. They have the opportunity to review organizational and time-management practices, employee interaction skills and team meetings. The supervisors selected to be "shadowed" should be effective role models for the new supervisor.

COACHING AND/OR MENTORING

Every new supervisor should be assigned a mentor. This may be his or her immediate manager, but does not need to be. The role of the mentor is to meet with new supervisors and team leaders on a regular basis for the first several months in the position, as well as making themselves available on an as-needed basis. Mentors provide experienced insights on any challenges faced by new supervisors, as well as counseling and career direction. It is best to have a formal process in place to ensure all necessary ground is covered. In addition, supervisors should be paired with a representative from Human Resources for staff issues. This is especially important for new supervisors who are learning policies and procedures connected with interviewing, hiring, performance management, disciplinary actions and termination.

Source: Dan Lowe, Lowe Consulting Group, GroupLCG@aol.com

resentative handling complaints in the newspaper's circulation department.

Weinhardt cites job knowledge as a key advantage of having spent time on the front line, and adds that "You also know the people you'll be supervising, and what their strengths and weaknesses are.

Yet, there can be disadvantages associated with internal advancement. For instance, Shimota points out that agents who haven't worked in other call centers, may not question long-standing policies and procedures as an outsider might. "Just because something has been done a certain way in the past, doesn't mean we always have to do it that way," she says. "When you hire staff from other companies, they bring with them the culture and processes of those companies—and you can often make great advances by knowing how other companies do something."

There's also the delicate issue of supervising former peers and learning how to set interpersonal boundaries, says Weinhardt.

Karly Fisher, fellow team leader at the London Free Press, agrees. "Sometimes people with whom you were once a peer may think they can take advantage of you," she says. "But the benefits of knowing the job and having done it yourself far outweigh that. You hit the ground running."

Chapter 4

Define Supervisory Roles and Responsibilities

Before you can begin assessing your agents for leadership potential, it's important to step back and consider the supervisor or team leader role. "Develop a detailed job description that specifically outlines what you want people in that position to do," says Langstone. "It should be broken down by percentage of time to be spent in each particular task."

Each team leader at American Express Financial Services' Mutual Fund and Certificate Transactions call centers oversees approximately 15 agents. The day-to-day floor management occupies 70 to 80 percent of their time, says Shimota. Team leaders are also responsible for monitoring at least two calls per team member each month and sharing feedback with the individuals. (A separate quality group also monitors five calls per month per agent.)

The remainder of their time is spent working on special projects or acting as liaisons with other areas of the company, responsible for bringing information back to the centers, as well as providing input for future decisions, says Shimota.

Team leaders at Prudential Financial's two call center sites play a key role in agent development, according to Joanne Herrman, claims office manager.

"We have very specific goals and objectives that are communicated to new-hires and agents in monthly feedback sessions," Herrman says. "The supervisor's role is to communicate those and to define them in objective and observable behaviors. They then link those objectives and behaviors to the overall organizational strategy so that agents understand what it is and how the job they do impacts the bottom line financials of the company."

Team leaders also conduct call-quality training during new-hire orientation as well as in monthly, ongoing feedback sessions.

Importantly, team leaders are responsible for maintaining the culture, as well. "They're responsible for being objective and supportive in their communication and for creating an environment of respect and support. Employee satisfaction is a key objective that we have in our call center," Herrman says.

Supporting the front line is also key. "Our main focus is to make sure we're doing everything we can to maximize everybody's performance so we can meet our individual and departmental objectives," says Team Leader Fisher.

Selecting the Right Individuals for Leadership Development

Once the supervisor's role is defined, you can develop a profile of competencies and skills required to perform those duties. While, certainly, many supervisory skills can be acquired, following are a few key traits that managers seek in potential leaders.

• **Adaptability.** "Look for individuals who can function in a variety of environments and situations, no matter what comes up," suggests Carol Horner, president of Synchronicity Training & Development in Council Bluffs, Iowa.

• **Problem-solving and decision making skills.** "They go hand-in-hand," says Shimota. "Supervisors should have a deeper understanding of why certain guidelines exist," and be able to consider various options and decide on the best solutions for customers and the company.

• **Interpersonal skills.** "Listening skills are important to be an effective coach," Shimota says. So, too, are the abilities to build rapport with colleagues and subordinates, knowing how to ask the right questions and being able to tailor communication styles to individual needs, adds Langstone.

• **Objectivity.** "Look for people who can be analytical and objective when evaluating agents and situations," says Herrman.

• **Emotional balance.** Good candidates for supervisory positions should be well-balanced emotionally, says Horner. "They shouldn't be easily stressed or frustrated with others."

• **Professional demeanor.** Herrman defines this as the ability to be supportive and maintain confidentiality when dealing with individuals and sensitive issues.

• **Ability to influence others.** "Leaders need to be able to develop frontline staff, and solicit from them creative thinking and innovation," says Langstone. These are also the people who are willing to share what they know with their colleagues.

And importantly, consider those agents who have a passion for the job,

Chapter 4

Langstone adds. "Make sure a potential candidate is connected to the job, and feels a personal investment in the organization's success."

The desire to move ahead is often the key indicator of whether an agent will excel in a leadership position. "Keep in mind that they may not have a real interest in becoming a supervisor," says Horner. "But there may not be any other option to improve their status in the organization."

MONITORING IS KEY ROLE FOR SUPERVISORS/TEAM LEADERS

Monitoring call center agents is a critical task for supervisors and team leaders in most call centers, according to ICMI's *Call Center Monitoring Study II Final Report*. The study, involving 735 call centers of various sizes and industries, found that four out of five call centers delegate that responsibility to supervisors/team leaders. One in two centers have managers monitor calls, while four out of 10 centers have an internal quality assurance specialist perform the task. The study also found that:

• Approximately three-quarters of the call centers studied provide formal evaluation/coaching to those who conduct the monitoring—an increase of more than 10 percent from two years ago. Call center size impacts the likelihood that formal evaluation/coaching will be provided to those monitoring. For instance, while only 62 percent of centers with fewer than 50 agents provide evaluation/coaching, the percentage increases with size: 71 percent of centers with 50-99 agents; 73 percent, 100-199 agents; 84 percent, 200-399 agents; and 87 percent of centers with 400 or more agents provide evaluation/coaching to those who conduct the monitoring.

• Sixty-two percent of respondents indicated that those who conduct the monitoring feel they do not have enough time to provide effective monitoring/feedback. That figure has improved since 1999 when just over 50 percent of call center respondents felt that way.

Source: Call Center Monitoring Study II Final Report, *ICMI Inc., www.icmi.com.*

Career Opportunities Well above PAR at PharmaCare Call Centers

by Greg Levin

Unhappy call center agents often point to a lack of job diversity and minimal growth opportunities as the reason for their dissatisfaction. Those agents obviously haven't worked for PharmaCare recently.

In 1999, PharmaCare successfully implemented Professional Advancement Requirements (PARs)—a program specifically aimed at enhancing agent development and expanding the career path at the company's call centers in Lincoln, R.I. and Fairfield, Ohio. PARs features a variety of job levels and specialized tracks, each with focused requirements for training and performance. As agents advance, they not only pick up a bigger paycheck, they become more empowered to make important decisions and to head up or assist with a wide range of projects and strategic tasks.

The result is a happier and more productive front-line staff, who—unlike agents in many companies—view the call center as much more than just a transitional or static job.

"Overall, I believe the PARs program has been what has kept us in the competition in the industry," says Annmaric Jenkins, manager of Call Centers for PharmaCare. "It has made a tremendous impact when interviewing people for possible positions, and even though the starting pay is minimal, there are significant opportunities for one to have a career in the call center."

A Closer Peak at PARs

Five principle job levels form the backbone of PharmaCare's PARs program:

1. **Trainee.** This is what all new-hires start out as in the call center. Trainees' primary responsibilities are to observe and learn mail service procedures and customer service operations. Once they are on the phones, trainees are responsible for assessing and collecting data from customers to resolve prescription status issues, as well as for handling billing inquiries, requests for enrollment

materials and phone-in prescription refills.

JOB REQUIREMENTS:

- One to two years of customer service work experience
- Highly developed work ethics
- Good communication skills
- Strong interpersonal, organizational and analytical skills
- Computer proficiency
- Pharmacy Tech skills desirable

2. **Level I.** Level I agents have similar responsibilities as Trainees, but—because they have had more time on the job (trainees usually become Level I agents after about six to eight months)—they are expected to perform at a higher level. In addition, Level I agents are responsible for assisting customers with using the Web to find the information they seek.

JOB REQUIREMENTS (IN ADDITION TO THE CENTER'S CORE REQUIREMENTS DESCRIBED IN THE TRAINEE POSITION):

- Initial RxClaim experience or equivalent

3. **Level II Specialist.** Once agents reach the Level II Specialist position, their job begins to diversify. In addition to doing what Level I agents do, Level II Specialists calculate price quote estimates; support mail service Level I issues; handle RxClaim HelpDesk calls as needed; approve prior authorizations when appropriate; and participate in special projects.

JOB REQUIREMENTS (IN ADDITION TO THE CENTER'S CORE REQUIREMENTS):

- One or more years experience on CDS Elite System or equivalent experience
- Six months RxClaim experience or equivalent

4. **Level III Analyst.** These are advanced agents who, in addition to their customer support responsibilities on the phones/Internet (as well as the HelpDesk), are involved in a variety of projects and supervisory tasks. Level III Analysts help to organize and oversee self-directed work teams; observe less experienced agents for quality assurance; assist with coaching and training staff; and even help prepare management reports.

Chapter 4

JOB REQUIREMENTS (IN ADDITION TO THE CENTER'S CORE REQUIREMENTS):

- Two to three years of customer service work experience
- Two or more years experience on CDS Elite System or equivalent experience
- One year RxClaim experience or equivalent
- Strong leadership skills
- Excellent written/verbal communication skills

5. Team Leader. While Team leaders still handle customer contacts, a large part of their time is spent working on off-phone tasks/projects and helping other staff to improve. As PharmaCare's Jenkins explains, "The Team Leader position is filled by the 'best of our best.' The people in this role—or those being groomed to be in this role—are extremely talented and skilled in our business. They have demonstrated their leadership abilities by leading by example, and less experienced agents look to them for guidance and direction." Jenkins adds that Team Leaders are qualified to fill in for supervisors who are away from the call center for whatever reason.

JOB REQUIREMENTS (IN ADDITION TO THE CENTER'S CORE REQUIREMENTS):

- Three to four years of customer service experience
- Strong dedication and leadership skills
- Two to three years TechRx and RxClaim experience
- Excellent written and verbal communication skills
- Good stress management skills
- Experience in managing multiple priorities
- Ability to work with minimal supervision
- Familiarity with call center technologies preferred

Moving on Up

The PARs program is introduced to agents as soon as they start working at PharmaCare. Team Leaders carefully explain the details and objectives of the program to new-hires during their first one-on-one meeting. Each agent then receives an "Individual Development Plan" (IDP) to ensure that they get off to

Chapter 4

a good start in the program and that they understand the minimum requirements they need to achieve before they can advance. "The IDP is a roadmap of what the agent is working on and how long it is anticipated before they achieve their goal," explains Jenkins.

Originally, the center set strict timelines for each job level, but has since implemented a more flexible policy. For instance, a Trainee used to have to work on the phone floor for a minimum of six months before being considered for a Level I position, and a Level I needed to wait at least a year to become a Level II. Today, however, how quickly an agent advances depends on that individual. "For example," Jenkins says, "we have a young gentleman who had only been with us for one year before we promoted him to a Level III. This is the fastest that anyone has ever progressed through the PARs program." She adds that the center is currently grooming that talented agent for a Team Leader position.

To help agents acquire the skills and knowledge they need to advance, the center uses a self-paced training method that features comprehensive workbooks. Each agent must pass a test for each workbook they complete. Occasionally, an outside seminar may be used to supplement the in-house training provided for the higher job levels, says Jenkins. "We are currently developing our own in-house coaching and leadership training that will be incorporated into the Level III requirements." The call center has also recently purchased the International Customer Service Association's (ICSA) "Through the Customer's Eyes" certification program, which will be added to the Level II requirements.

In addition to formal training, regular monitoring and coaching sessions help agents to develop and hone the skills they need to move up in the call center ranks. During feedback sessions, Team Leaders and Supervisors go over the agent's current IDP and discuss what the agent is doing well, as well as where and how they can improve.

While coaching and training play a key part in preparing agents for new positions, experience "in the trenches" is the most important mode of learning, says Jenkins. "The biggest tool we use is on-the-job training. For example, if a member sends in a complaint and asks for resolution, we will ask an agent looking to be promoted to research the issue and present the supervisor with how they would handle it. Then, depending on the severity of the complaint, we may have the agent call the member back while we monitor the call."

Every move an agent makes up the PARs ladder is accompanied by an increase in pay—ranging from symbolic to significant—which helps to inspire staff to stay in the call center and continually acquire more skills. "When an agent advances from a Trainee to Level I, the [pay] increase is not significant," says Jenkins. "However, when an agent advances to a Level II, the increase is over $1.50 more per hour." An agent's level also has an impact on how much "merit pay" they earn each year. "Since our merit increases are based on a percentage of what you make," Jenkins says, "the higher your base salary, the higher your merit increase will be year to year."

Opportunities Expanding

To further expand career opportunities in the call center, PharmaCare recently added several specialized positions that higher level agents can strive for. These positions include:

• Quality Assurance Analyst—responsible for monitoring agent calls and tracking measurements for quality/training purposes. Agents must achieve Level II status to qualify for this position, and exhibit excellent listening and coaching skills.

• Workload Planner—analyzes volume forecasts from the workforce management system to create effective short- and long-term staff schedules. This is an advanced position that requires ample call center experience and familiarity with workforce management systems, and thus is likely to be filled by somebody at the Team Leader level.

• Call Allocator—in charge of real-time resource management and monitoring using complex scheduling software and phone systems. This position provides support to the Workload Planner to ensure staffing/scheduling success. Requirements for this position are similar to those for the Workload Planner position.

Chapter 4

According to Jenkins, PharmaCare plans to add some additional specialized positions to the lineup, including Web Team Analyst, who will investigate online customer complaints and respond via email and Web chat; Call Center Support Leader, who will supervise programs designed to advance the objectives of the call center; and Call Center Trainer, who will be responsible for planning, developing and conducting all agent training.

Rewards and Challenges

All these opportunities have helped to foster a high level of enthusiasm—as well as a strong commitment to the call center—among PharmaCare's frontline staff. In fact, in 2001, the call center didn't lose a single Level II employee.

Level II Specialist Michele Roesch loves how PARs has enabled him to control his destiny in the call center while at the same time providing him with the support he needs.

"The PARs program allows me to take responsibility for some of my additional job training," says Roesch. "By working with my supervisor to set goals, I can work step by step through the PARs. As I master each step I become stronger in my work skills and, in doing so, become more valuable to my employer. Future advancement and pay increases become more motivating when I have some control over meeting the required goals."

Agents aren't the only ones who benefit from the PARs program. With agents participating in a diverse range of tasks and continuously learning more advanced skills, the call center's supervisors are able to concentrate on what *they* do best. "One of the benefits realized from implementing the program is that supervisors' time has been freed up to focus more on coaching and developing," explains Jenkins. "Since the levels take on more responsibility, they are seen as the experts on the floor. They are used in handling escalated calls and issue resolution."

While the program is creating a lot of positive change, things haven't always been so rosy. For instance, the company initially struggled to fully gain agent acceptance, says Jenkins. "At first, the more experienced agents did not take to

Chapter 4

the program. They felt they were being overlooked and not recognized for their experience they had already put in. After explaining to them that they control their own earning potential with the company, the agents gave their buy-in."

Growing pains associated with the PARs have also created challenges. "Because of how our environment is constantly changing, we have struggled to keep up with it," says Jenkins, who adds that the company is constantly working to revitalize the program and keep it fresh.

Spreading the Success

Despite the challenges, PARs is still going strong and gaining ample recognition companywide. In fact, PharmaCare is currently planning to introduce the program to its call center in Fort Worth, Texas.

Other companies interested in improving agent retention and performance should consider implementing something similar, says Jenkins. And she's doing her part to make that happen—giving presentations on the PAR program at seminars and conferences, including Call Center Week. And when speaking about creating a call center career path, she offers some key advice that falls into the category of "lessons learned."

"Looking back, I would suggest that professionals always seek buy-in from their employees. For example, what do they think constitutes a Level I, Level II or Level III?" She also recommends that the program be clearly defined from beginning to end prior to its introduction to the floor, including how to incorporate the ever-changing needs of the business into the program. And finally, she advises, be sure that somebody is in charge. "Assign a team to the development, enhancement and maintenance of the program's integrity."

Follow this advice, and the faces in your call center will likely become more and more familiar.

"We are seeing many employees celebrate their second, third, fourth and even fifth anniversaries with the call center," says Jenkins. "This has been the biggest benefit of the program. I believe that the employees really see their jobs as careers rather than a dead-end position."

Chapter 4

From CSR to Workflow Architect: A Career Path Success Story

by Lori Bocklund

Sometimes, probably more often than you would think, a wonderful call center "people" story lies just beneath the surface of a technology story. This is one such story.

I teach courses on call center technology. I love to discuss examples of successful deployments of the latest, greatest things. Recently, I was talking to a group of call center professionals about a CTI-enabled (computer telephony integration) customer relationship management (CRM) solution with powerful workflows. One of my "hot buttons" about the deployment of these types of technologies is the need to have someone who is close to the business involved with the technology--not just the technologists. As I related an example of a specific young man's progression from frontline CSR to supervisor to applied technology support to workflow architect, my esteemed colleagues pointed out what a wonderful people story it was.

I agree. Every call center struggles with the continual battle against agent turnover, and is constantly on the lookout for ways to create a rewarding, challenging career path for skilled staff. It's important to make visible these success stories to stir the thinking of others in the business and perhaps create more successes. My hope is that this profile gets passed around and posted, and inspires managers to create more opportunities—and CSRs to seize them.

Let's Meet Michael McDonald

Michael McDonald works for Riggs Bank, a regional bank in the Washington, D.C. area. He's one of the sharp, interesting and interested people on whom call centers depend.

McDonald has a B.S./B.A. in human resource management from American University. Like many of us, he didn't foresee a call center career while in college. In fact, he wanted to go into the securities business, working with 401k or other investment plans. He even started down that path, obtaining the necessary insurance and trading licenses, and working for an investment firm.

It was in 1993 that McDonald really began his career in the call center at Riggs Bank, where he was hired as a sales and service representative (SSR). Back then, the call center was small and had no supervisors. Instead, McDonald and several other SSRs took turns supervising on a volunteer basis. He had seized his first opportunity.

Within two years, McDonald became one of the first official supervisors in the center, managing a staff of more than 40. He provided training, monitoring and coaching to the staff. He even served as editor of the weekly and monthly

---

MICHAEL MCDONALD'S KEYS TO SUCCESS

How can you be (or develop) a Michael McDonald within your own call center?

McDonald offers the following keys to call center career path success:

• Take all opportunities offered to you. Some duties may not be glamorous, but they build your reputation as a team player and as someone who is dependable and trustworthy. That positions you for the next opportunity when it comes along.

• Have other interests outside of work that help you to grow. McDonald loves to travel, makes time for community and volunteer work, and is always seeking additional education. His interests enhance his skills and resume and help him to continually grow, which keeps him ready and eager for the next challenge.

McDonald also offers the following advice, which has made his Riggs' experience highly positive. These four suggestions will help anyone to succeed in a contact center:

• Work with friends. McDonald first came into the call center environment through a friend's recommendation. But, beyond that, he considers his coworkers to be his friends. That makes it a great place to be every day, he says.

• Be open to change. Change is always happening. So watch, wait and be ready to embrace it when it arrives, and help it to succeed.

• Be a team player. Team players get the opportunities. Why? They're the ones to whom people turn when the center needs to make something happen.

• Focus on the customer. No matter what your role—operations, technology or a combination of both—focusing on the customer is key to success. If you can always keep them (and their needs) in mind, what you do will be successful.

call center newsletters. Another opportunity created—and seized.

McDonald continued to proactively expand his call center knowledge and skills. He eventually became the systems administrator and assistant manager. In this new role, he became more involved with the center's technology, although his responsibilities still focused largely on management and operations. Because of his unique grasp of both operations management and technology, McDonald also became the liaison between the call center and its internal/external partners for technology projects. He used and applied call center technologies, including reporting tools, a logging system and a workforce management system. He also trained supervisors on how to effectively use reporting tools. Within the company, people began to seek McDonald's input before purchasing technology.

What's a Workflow Architect?

The most recent development in McDonald's career path was his promotion to "workflow architect." His responsibilities include: developing requirements, writing workflows using a rules-based system, testing, moving workflows into production, day-to-day system administration, data security and audits. While this new position sounds vastly different from being a frontline CSR, McDonald's call center experience was critical to his success.

McDonald's key role as a workflow architect is to help develop applications that will benefit the call center and its customers—through increased efficiency, as well as by enabling agents to do more on behalf of the customer. The job was created when Riggs Bank embarked on a project to install a CTI solution to be used for inbound and outbound workflows and call flows, and which would enable call routing and delivery, screen pops, tracking and reporting, triggering scripts and more. When Riggs implemented the solution, it changed the whole look and feel of the contact center systems and processes. New screens had to be designed, new information was made available to CSRs and new information was created on every contact.

Chapter 4

Call Center Credentials Form a Solid Foundation

So imagine you are going to roll out a similar type of project in your call center involving elaborate process and technology changes. Who better to be a part of the design team than someone with McDonald's credentials? He brought to the team an intimate, firsthand knowledge of what it's like to be on the phones with customers using the systems, while trying to meet all of the performance goals for efficiency and customer-focused service. He also understood the potential ripple effect of the technology project, as well as what would and wouldn't work in the trenches.

But that's just the design side of things. As we all know, implementation is another story. McDonald was not a programmer—he was from operations. What he had, though, was the foundation to make the leap—intelligence, interest, eagerness and a willingness to learn.

McDonald was trained on the product (Pegasystems), and soon was writing workflows in the programming tools, writing HTML, using and customizing Active X controls and JavaScript. He worked alongside "true programmers," from both the vendor's organization and his own company's IT shop. He learned about CTI and client/server architectures, databases and switch-routing software. His peers often found him with a *JavaScript for Dummies* book on his desk, digging for a deeper understanding of the tools and capabilities at his disposal, and how he could best apply them to the business needs.

Teaching Staff to Fish

McDonald's transition into workflow architect was not without pain. Most of us are familiar with the Chinese proverb: "Give a man a fish, and he eats for a day. Teach a man to fish, and he eats for a lifetime." The first six months in his new role, McDonald was learning how to fish with close assistance from the vendor's resources. Other Riggs' staff were also brought in to assist, including some with programming experience (but not with experience with Pegasystems' product) and some additional "rookies."

McDonald's new role also requires him to work in new and different ways

Chapter 4

than before. Although he continues to report to the call center operation, his role has shifted to IT, which, he has discovered, is a completely different mind-set from that in the call center.

Leadership Sets the Direction

Another crucial dimension to a successful career path is leadership. McDonald attributes some of his success to strong leadership in the call center.

Throughout his development and growth, his call center manager acted as a true mentor, creating opportunities for him (and others) and giving him the chance to succeed. McDonald's manager also had vision and focus for the call center and what it needed to achieve, defining the projects that help to create career opportunities.

Leaders who take a leap of faith with an employee are critical to the success of individuals as well as the call center. Riggs has created this culture of opportunity. In fact, some of McDonald's peers have progressed to roles as training coordinators, marketing and data warehousing, and other positions across the bank.

Where to Go from Here?

With all of his accomplishments so far, McDonald isn't ready to rest on his laurels yet. He has taken several programming classes in the last two years and is planning to get a master's degree in information systems or telecommunications. He feels this goal will enable him to reach the next level in applying his business knowledge to technical applications and solutions that meet user and customer needs. It will also help him to further grow his collaboration with his new peers in the IT department.

McDonald enjoys his interdisciplinary career—"the best of both worlds," as he puts it. He welcomes the new challenges that arrive daily, and enjoys seeing the benefits that technology brings to the business. He relishes the opportunities that change presents to learn and grow. Now that's a success story!

Chapter 4

Chapter 5: Call Center Satire

Motivating and fairly compensating call center staff is serious business... so is being able to laugh about such topics once in a while. Here are a couple articles for comic relief.

A Brief Guide to Progressive Agent Incentives and Recognition

By Greg Levin

Numerous studies have shown that agents who feel overstressed, underpaid and unappreciated tend to treat customers poorly, make numerous errors and are three times more likely than happy agents to set a supervisor on fire. In fact, of the 15 incidents where call center supervisors caught fire last year, 14 were caused by agents with low morale (the 15th incident was the result of a vacationing supervisor who got careless during a volcano expedition).

Call centers without innovative incentives and recognition practices often incur astronomical turnover rates and poor customer loyalty. Yet few centers have implemented truly progressive practices that inspire agents to achieve organizational objectives and to forget the fact that they are chained to cubicles.

Here are a few examples of what I believe are the most creative and promising motivational tactics around. (Note: Some of these ideas are still a bit unrefined. You may want to first test them out on lab mice or a select group of agents you particularly dislike.)

Executive Suites for Top Performers

You can't expect agents to feel proud and continually meet the high demands placed on them if they continue to be shackled to cramped workstations in a warehouse environment. You need to show them that they are just as valuable to the company as the CEO. That's why I suggest building an octagonal-shaped call center where your top eight performers each get to work in a corner office.

Agents will knock themselves out on the phones to earn the right to occupy one of these "executive suites." To sweeten the pot and to provide agents with a real feeling of power, you can also give those who attain "agent executive" status a key to the executive washroom, permit them to speak to customers via speakerphone and give them the right to completely ignore the rest of the call center staff.

It's best to rotate top performers in and out of the executive suites on a weekly or monthly basis. Longer stays may cause agents to get cocky and start recommending staffing cuts or negotiating mergers.

Radical Title Change

Another great way to make agents feel important and valued is to change their job titles to something that commands more respect.

Instead of the bland "agent" or "rep," try something creative like "Headset Honcho," "Contact King," "Queue Queen" or the increasingly popular, "The Artist Formerly Known as Operator."

You'd be amazed at how a radical title change can impact motivation and performance. For example, a catalog call center in Eau de Formage, Wis., recently conducted a revealing experiment where it separated agents into three groups, giving the agents in each group a different title: 1) "Agent"; 2) "Customer Specialist"; and 3) "Service Overlord."

The results were remarkable: The "Agent" group achieved mediocre service levels, reported high turnover and set two supervisors on fire. The "Customer Specialist Group" faired better—achieving average service levels with a moderate rate of turnover and setting only one supervisor on fire. In comparison, the "Service Overlord" group exceeded all service level objectives, had zero turnover and quickly extinguished the three supervisor fires.

Spell-Based Pay Program

Two unfortunate call center facts:

- Most agent salaries wouldn't even pay for one of the CEO's golf clubs; and
- Most agents can't even spell "CEO" when writing customer email.

One of the best ways to enhance agent wages (and retention rates) while, at the same time, improving your center's email response quality is to introduce a formal "spell-based pay" program.

Here's how it works: For every correctly spelled word in an agent's email response, you pay them 5 cents—or 1 cent if you manage a service bureau. Not only will such a program enable agents to earn some much-needed additional money and inspire them to improve, it will greatly reduce the chances of your call center being paid an angry visit by editors from Merriam-Webster.

The only real drawback of a spell-based pay program is that as agents' writing improves, they may earn enough money to buy a newspaper and find other job opportunities in the area.

Chapter 5

Spicing Up the Agent Image
By Greg Levin

Many call center professionals have told me that they are struggling more than ever to attract qualified agent applicants. My typical piece of advice, "Wear something sexy"—which, by the way, used to get big laughs—now causes managers to merely growl and tell me to grow up. They're fed up with having to recruit from a shallow labor pool, and even my sophisticated wit isn't enough to get them to crack a smile anymore.

The big problem is the negative image that most young people have of call center work: sitting in small, gray cubicles while wearing an uncomfortable headset and answering call after call after call for hours on end, with little room for advancement. But that's such a distorted view. For instance, some cubicles today are a nice shade of blue.

Okay, let's face it, as rewarding as call center work may be, on the surface it's not that alluring to college graduates or others with strong communication skills and serious debt. Here are some suggestions to help spice-up the industry image and enhance the chances of you having to tell alumni from schools like Stanford and Brown that you'll keep their resume on file in case an agent position opens up.

1. Provide "alternative" headsets. Many young people feel that wearing a headset is a sign of failure, an indication that they are just a lowly "operator" lacking any real skills. They fail to realize that 1) being a call center agent requires numerous important skills; 2) even CEOs wear headsets during long calls to avoid stiff necks; and 3) four out of five medical doctors surveyed say that wearing a headset significantly decreases the chances of having a wasp fly into your ear while on the job.

But rather than try to overcome the general public's negative view of headsets, why not replace the devices with something that doesn't really look like a headset. For example, you could decorate each headset with fake diamonds, rubies and emeralds. Then, whenever you meet reluctant applicants who feel they are "above" call center work, you can tell them they'll get to wear a bejeweled crown to fit their royal self-image.

2. Break up the monotony. Most people are turned off by call center work because the thought of handling calls from the average Joe all day long makes them yawn. They want something more exciting and unpredictable. I say give them what they want. Do creative things like occasionally hire an actor to play a disgruntled customer who runs into the call center screaming obscenities and threatening the lives of any agent who moves from their seat. This will not only get staff's adrenaline pumping and make them tell their friends (potential applicants) how invigorating their job is, it will reduce the amount of "wandering" agents engage in, thus improving adherence-to-schedule statistics.

Other easy ways to inject excitement into the agents' call center routine include 1) sponsoring unannounced "nude supervisor" days; 2) releasing a rabid wolverine on the phone floor; and 3) moving the call center to Rio during Carnival.

3. Create a TV sitcom about agents in a call center. One of the best ways to attract young people to call center work is to make it the subject of a hit comedy TV sitcom, preferably starring Chandler from *Friends* as the zany lead agent. I urge call center professionals throughout the industry to get together and create such a show, and call it something like *Mad About Queue* or *Ain't Life a Kick in the Headset*. All that's needed is about 10 good-looking mediocre actors wearing cool clothes, a New York City or Los Angeles setting, some call center props and, of course, a rabid wolverine or two.

Each episode could highlight typical call center occurrences, with a little embellishment to enhance ratings. For instance, the pilot episode could be about how the agents—struggling to handle the center's call volume—kidnap the CEO's wife and golf clubs until he agrees to staffing increases.

I recommend contacting the head of the Fox Television Network to get this baby on TV. There should be no problem winning his approval, provided that you follow the Fox formula and promise that all characters will sleep with one another before the end of the first season.

Note: If all else fails in your attempts to attract hordes of agent applicants, consider paying off the Surgeon General to declare that NOT handling dozens of calls a day from customers can cause baldness and bad breath.

Index

Publication Dates

How to Reach the Publisher

We would love to hear from you. How could this book be improved? Has it been helpful? No comments are off limits. You can reach us at:

Mailing Address: Call Center Press, a division of ICMI, Inc.
P.O. Box 6177
Annapolis, MD 21401

Telephone: 410-267-0700, 800-672-6177

Fax: 410-267-0962

Email: icmi@icmi.com

Web site: www.icmi.com

About Incoming Calls Management Institute

ICMI Inc. is a global leader in call center consulting, training, publications and membership services. ICMI's mission is to help call centers (contact centers, help desks, customer care, support centers) achieve operational excellence and superior business results. Through the dedication and experience of its team, uncompromised objectivity and results-oriented vision, ICMI has earned a reputation as the industry's most trusted resource for:

- Consulting
- Seminars
- Publications
- Management Tools
- Conferences and Networking Events
- Professional Membership

Based in Annapolis, Maryland, ICMI was established in 1985 and was first to develop and deliver management training customized for call centers. Through constant innovation and research, ICMI's training has become the industry's gold standard, and is recommended by 99.3% of those managers who have experienced its value first-hand. Over the years, ICMI has become the industry's leading provider of membership services with an impressive line-up of call center management resources, including instant access to prominent research, expert advice and career development tools, and a networking forum that spans more than 40 countries worldwide. ICMI is not associated with, owned or subsidized by any industry supplier—its only source of funding is from those who use its services. For more information about ICMI, visit www.icmi.com, or call 800-672-6177 (410-267-0700).

Author Biographies*

Brad Cleveland is President and CEO of Incoming Calls Management Institute (ICMI), and Publisher of *Call Center Management Review*. He has delivered keynotes, seminars and consulting services in over 25 countries, and is co-author of the best-selling book, *Call Center Management on Fast Forward*.

Lori Bocklund is President of independent consulting firm Strategic Contact, and is ICMI's Technology Management Professional Interest Area Advisor. She is a prominent speaker at leading industry events, a frequent contributor to *Call Center Management Review* and co-author of the book *Call Center Technology Demystified*.

Dan Coen is call center manager for Blue Shield of California's call center in Los Angeles. He is a published author as well as a management workshop leader. Dan specializes in cultivating agent teams and developing proven incentive/compensation plans to enhance quality and productivity.

Christian Ellis is a senior consultant in Sibson & Co.'s Cary, North Carolina office and helps call centers enhance performance via their human capital.

*Author information is current for the publication date of the article (see page 171).

Leslie Hansen Harps is a freelance business writer specializing in customer service and call centers. She is the former president of the Customer Service Institute, and author of several books.

Susan Hash is the editor-in-chief of *Call Center Management Review*. She has been a business journalist/writer for more than 15 years, and has received several notable journalism awards for reporting on the customer service industry.

Mark G. Haug, Ph.D., J.D. teaches graduate and undergraduate courses in operations management, business law, statistics and leadership at the University of Kansas School of Business. He is also a partner with and general counsel to Oread Consulting Group.

Elizabeth Hawk is a principal and one of the leaders of the organizational performance and rewards practice at Sibson & Co., a firm specializing in call center effectiveness and compensation consulting.

Chris Heide is a professional writer specializing in customer service, sales and marketing issues. His articles have appeared in a wide variety of trade and general interest publications.

Greg Levin is the Creative Projects Specialist for ICMI. He is the former editor of *Call Center Management Review*, and author of ICMI's *Call Center Humor* book series.

Anne Nickerson is president of Call Center Coach, which provides call center professionals with comprehensive resources for human resource development processes.

Wanda Sitzer is executive vice president and co-founder of Initiatives Three Inc., a consulting firm specializing in phone and Web initiatives to improve customer service, marketing and sales management.

Fay Wilkinson is a senior partner with Questeq Learning Programs, an Orangeville, Ontario-based consulting firm specializing in helping call centers achieve their training and performance objectives. Fay has 30 years' experience in customer service and call centers, and has spoken at numerous industry conferences and seminars.

Order Form

QTY.	Item	Member Price	Price	Total
	Call Center Management On Fast Forward: Succeeding In Today's Dynamic Inbound Environment**	**$23.76**	$34.95	
	Call Center Technology Demystified: The No-Nonsense Guide to Bridging Customer Contact Technology, Operations and Strategy**	**$33.96**	$39.95	
	ICMI's Call Center Management Dictionary: The Essential Reference for Contact Center, Help Desk and Customer Care Professionals**	**$21.21**	$24.95	
	ICMI's Pocket Guide to Call Center Management Terms*	**$5.12**	$5.95	
	ICMI Handbook and Study Guide Series Module 1: People Management*** Module 2: Operations Management*** Module 3: Customer Relationship Management*** Module 4: Leadership and Business Management***	**$169.15 ea.**	$199.00 ea.	
	Topical Books: **The Best of *Call Center Management Review*** Call Center Recruiting and New Hire Training* Call Center Forecasting and Scheduling* Call Center Agent Motivation and Compensation* Call Center Agent Retention and Turnover*	**$14.41 ea.**	$16.95 ea.	
	Forms Books Call Center Sample Monitoring Forms** Call Center Sample Customer Satisfaction Forms Book**	**$42.46 ea.**	$49.95 ea.	
	Software QueueView: A Staffing Calculator—CD ROM* Easy Start™ Call Center Scheduler Software—CD-ROM*	**$41.65** **$254.15**	$49.95 $299.00	
	Call Center Humor: The Best of *Call Center Management Review* Volume 3*	**$8.45**	$9.95	
	The Call Centertainment Book*	**$7.61**	$8.95	
	Shipping & Handling @ $5.00 per US shipment, plus .50¢ per* item, $1.00 per** item and $2.00 per*** item. Additional charges apply to shipments outside the US.			
	Tax (5% MD residents, 7% GST Canadian residents)			
	TOTAL (US dollars)			

Please contact us for quantity discounts
For more information on our products, please visit **www.icmi.com**

❑ Please send me a free issue of *Call Center Management Review* (ICMI's journal for members) and information on ICMI's publications, services and membership.

Please ship my order and/or information to:

Name _____

Title _____

Industry _____

Company _____

Address _____

City _____ State _____ Postal Code _____

Telephone ( ) _____

Fax ( ) _____

Email _____

Method of Payment (if applicable)

❑ Check enclosed (Make payable to ICMI Inc.; U.S. Dollars only)

❑ Charge to: ❑ American Express ❑ MasterCard ❑ Visa

Account No. _____

Expiration Date _____

Name on Card _____

Fax order to: 410-267-0962
call us at: 800-672-6177 or 410-267-0700
order online at: www.icmi.com
or mail order to: ICMI Inc.
P.O. Box 6177, Annapolis, MD 21401